Lost F

of Vietnam

Books previously published

by Dr. Haha Lung:

The Ancient Art of Strangulation (1995)
Assassin! Secrets of the Cult of Assassins (1997)
The Ninja Craft (1997)
Knights of Darkness (1998)

Written with Christopher B. Prowant:

Shadowhand: Secrets of Ninja Taisavaki (2000)
The Black Science: Ancient and Modern Techniques of Ninja Mind Manipulation (2001)

Written as "Ralf Dean Omar":

Death on Your Doorstep: 101 Weapons in the Home (1993)
Prison Killing Techniques: Blade, Bludgeon & Bomb (2001)

Written as "Dirk Skinner":

Street Ninja: Ancient Secrets for Mastering Today's Mean Streets (1995)
X-Treme Boxing: Secrets of the Savage Street Boxer (2002) with Christopher B. Prowant

Lost Fighting Arts
of Vietnam

Dr. Haha Lung

CITADEL PRESS
Kensington Publishing Corp.
www.kensingtonbooks.com

CITADEL PRESS BOOKS are published by

Kensington Publishing Corp.
850 Third Avenue
New York, NY 10022

Illustrations by Dr. Haha Lung

All Kensington titles, imprints, and distributed lines are available at special quantity discounts for bulk purchases for sales promotions, premiums, fund-raising, educational, or institutional use. Special book excerpts or customized printings can also be created to fit specific needs. For details, write or phone the office of the Kensington special sales manager: Kensington Publishing Corp., 850 Third Avenue, New York, NY 10022, attn: Special Sales Department; phone 1-800-221-2647.

First printing: June 2006

10 9 8 7 6 5 4 3 2 1

Printed in the United States of America

Library of Congress Control Number: 2002110953

ISBN 0-8065-2760-9

Dedication

To Christopher B. Prowant, Master Eddie Harris, Master Wan Tzu, Charles Shumway and Geoffrey Beer. And to Lenox Cramer SF, a good warrior in a bad war.

———————

Contents

Disclaimer

It is not the intent of this book to disrespect any particular political faction, religious group, or crazed cadre who had a hand—overt or covert—in the development of Vietnamese history in general and the creation of the Cao Dai religion in particular.

I single out no one group for ridicule or blame.

When it comes to Vietnamese history, there's plenty enough ridicule and blame to go around!

The Cao Dai religion is alive and well today, both inside Vietnam and beyond her shores.

Each Cao Dai congregation around the world has its own distinct ways of worship, its own particular relationship with *Huyén Co*, "the Great Mystery."

Some of these groups teach the tradition of Vietnamese martial arts, some have other priorities.

If this author's recollections and translations of Vietnamese history and culture differ greatly from more accepted interpretations, no disrespect is intended. I hope none is taken.

But for any who might still be offended by this author's different sense of history, his confessed fascination with conspiracy, and his profound flair for the dramatic, I would remind them of the old Vietnamese adage:

"Di xa v'ê tha hô noi khoác." (Visitors from afar can lie with impunity.)

And for those still not satisfied, another response in Vietnamese is apropos:

"Do ma nhieu!" (Go fuck yourself.)

Dr. Haha Lung

Introduction
Vietnam "Jihad"?

I know what you're thinking. You're thinking that since you want to learn to "kick ass" with Cao Dai kung-fu, why should you have to take the time to study Vietnamese history and learn about all the sinister cults, conspiracies, and killer cadre that influenced Vietnamese history in general, and the development of the Cao Dai religion and Cao Dai kung-fu in particular?

You have a point.

If you're only interested in learning the *physical* application of Cao Dai kung-fu, feel free to jump to Section III of this book where you will find both armed and unarmed Cao Dai kung-fu fully described in easy-to-understand language.

So if all you study of this book is Section III, you will indeed learn many viable fighting techniques designed to both initiate the novice into the Asian fighting arts, while also giving even the most accomplished martial artist new takes on familiar kung-fu techniques.

However, if your ultimate goal is to *master* Cao Dai kung-fu, it's important to study the times and pressures that helped create this science of survival.

Because that's what Cao Dai kung-fu is: a *science* of survival.

———

In 1963, Vietnamese President Diem, a staunch Catholic, began systematically alienating all the other religions in Vietnam. As a direct result of Diem's actions, in short order, Diem was toppled in a coup and assassinated.

Ironically, of all the religious groups that would have loved to take a shot at Diem, it was "militant" Buddhists who get the credit for Diem's downfall — Buddhism, that most *peaceful* of religions.

1

If a religion as dedicated to non-violence as Buddhism could bring down a president, how much more of an effect could a suicidal religion have which demands their followers grip their "bible" in one hand and a ready blade for the "infidel" in the other?

After "Nine-Eleven" no one doubts the potential for terror that can vomit forth from the minds of crazed cultists.

Keeping current on the madness and motivations of such cults and crazies must form an intricate part of any *modern* self-defense and survival training.

Ignorance kills.

Prior to "Nine-Eleven" how many Americans knew what the Arabic word "Jihad" meant? On "Nine-Eleven" we all learned its meaning the hard way.

That *any* religion could spawn such cold conspiracy and devote so much of its energies to the creation of human killing machines may seem incredible to modern-day Americans.

But only to modern day Americans too lazy to heed George Santayana's warning.

Religion has always spawned the best killers: ancient *Zealots*, the medieval Muslim Assassin cult, Goddess-worshipping Indian *Thuggee* stranglers, the ruthless criminal *Triads* of China who proudly claim descent from Buddhist monks, and the dreaded ninja of Japan who can be traced back to mountain holy men called *Yamabushi*.

But the East has no monopoly on holy homicide. Let's not forget the Christian Crusades . . . and the Catholic Inquisition . . . and the Salem witch trials... and, well, you get the point.

That any religion would spur its adherents to homicide, or even encourage its members to master a deadly martial art, is unheard of — or at least no longer openly discussed — in the West today.

Yet not all religious groups who beat their plowshares into homicidal swords do so out of anger and ambition. Some are forced to do so only in order to survive intolerance and tumultuous times.

For example, when originally founded in the 16th century, the *Sikhs* of India were sworn to non-violence, but in order for their new religion to survive, overnight their marching orders did an about-face to *require* all Sikhs to study war.

So too with the mysterious Cao Dai religion of Vietnam.

The Cao Dai's purpose for encouraging the study of the art of war was two-fold: first, to save a valued Vietnamese tradition and cultural treasure—kung-fu. Second, and of more immediate concern, Cao Dai needed to protect its adherents during violet times.

From its inception, the Cao Dai have stared "violent times" in the face.

And so, out of necessity, the Cao Dai became warriors, mastering the art of war, patiently refining tried-and-true tactics and techniques already 1,000 years old.

As so, today, we benefit from their patience and perseverance.

That is, if we have equal patience and perseverance.

But in order to be thorough, to leave nothing to chance, we must study not just how blood is spilt on the open battlefield, but of equal importance, what goes on behind "The Black Curtain" of intrigue.

Not the keenest blade nor the thickest shield can protect us from that single drop of poison slipped into our distracted cup or, worse still, the seed of betrayal planted in a friend's ear.

During the Vietnam War, while American strategists debated how best to "win the hearts and minds" of the Vietnamese people, the Viet Cong were teaching their sappers how best to rip out the hearts and minds of Americans!

Fast-forward 30 years to the Middle East . . . have we really learned anything?

Whether a war is waged in a lush jungle or in a harsh desert, all wars have *two battlefields*, the physical one, and a just as deadly psychological battlefield.

We must be ready to combat our enemies on *both* these battle-fields.

True enough, learning *only* the physical aspects of Cao Dai kung-fu will indeed give you a keen-edged weapon with which to strike your enemy. But a good knife cuts both ways. Why sharpen your blade on only one edge? Why fill your arsenal only half way?

In the end, the more you know about life in general, the more options you have, the more *choices* — and chances! — for survival.

The more your *choices*, the better the odds victory will grace you with her smile.

This book gives you *choices*.

Section I
Chung Gai: "Spikes and Thorns"

Vietnamese history for the past few *thousand* years has been one of repeated invasion and near-constant warfare.

When asked for comment on their land's bloody history, Vietnamese shrug philosophically with *"Chung gai . . . spikes and thorns."*

Like so many other beautiful flowers, Vietnam has never been without its thorns.

Down through the centuries Vietnam's hardy peoples have grown accustomed to waking up to new — and all too often dangerous — challenges with each new dawn. Red sky in morning, traveler take warning!

While the ideal might be to seek a peaceful, uneventful life, to "stop and smell the roses" whenever possible, it is our having to watch out for the pricks of thorns that keeps us on our toes.

Thus, it is their own historical "spikes and thorns" that have allowed the peoples of Vietnam to grow strong, to resist the rage and ravage of wildfire and famine — whether natural disasters hurled by the will, wrath, and whimsy of the gods, or disasters brought about by the hatred and greed of their fellows.

It is not necessary to our purpose at hand that we devote ourselves to memorizing every nuance of the Vietnamese nation, its culture, language, etc. Nor is it necessary that we waste excessive time on cataloguing and critiquing every battle ever fought in Vietnam, every revolt and revolution brutally crushed.

However, it does behoove us to take time to acquire at least a basic general understanding of the land and its peoples, as well as a general chronology of its history, since both Vietnam's geographical realities and her historical events had great influence on the creation of the mysterious Cao Dai religion in general, while at the same time contributing tried-and-true tactics and techniques to Cao Dai kung-fu in particular.

Chapter One
Phuc Tinh: "Born Under a Lucky Star"

What is today Vietnam, consists of an area of 128,052 square miles, with a population of roughly 63 million, 90 percent of them Vietnamese. Thus the dominant language is also Vietnamese.

FYI: In Section II we will delve more deeply into the three major religions that have dominated Vietnamese history for centuries — Buddhism, Taoism, and Confucianism — with a smidgeon of Hinduism tossed into the stew for spice.

The land itself has long been looked at as three distinct regions: the Mekong Delta in the south, the heavily forested Annamite *Truong Son* mountain range that includes the plateaus of "the Central Highlands," and the narrow coastal strip that runs the length of the land from north to south.

These three regions correspond to the three historical "kingdoms" of Vietnam: Tonkin in the north, Annam in the central part of the country, and Cochin China in the south.

The people of the Central Highlands are today collectively known as "Montagnards" (French for "mountain folk"; Americans called them 'Yards, for short).

'Yards are descended from Malayo-Polynesian and Indo-Polynesian stock. Shorter and darker, 'Yards come from a different racial and cultural background than do the people Westerners today generally identify as "Vietnamese." These "Lowlanders" (as 'Yards refer to them) are, for the most part, descended from the Chinese.

FYI: Vietnamese today call 'Yards *Moi*, "savages." At one time Vietnamese school books characterized Montagnards as having a lot of body hair and long tails. (Dooley, 2000:46FN)

'Yards have some equally unflattering names for Lowlanders.

There are at least 32 distinct tribes of 'Yards, including the Rhade, Jarai, and Sedang. Warriors all.

By the way, 'Yards invented the crossbow — although the Chinese claim credit for it.

———

By 100 AD, Indian traders had already established trade routes to Cambodia and Laos, and were regularly visiting the coast of Vietnam. These traders were instrumental in spreading Indian economic influence, as well as exposing the indigenous people of the region to both Hindu and Buddhist religions.

FYI: Monuments with ancient Sanskrit (Indian) inscriptions can be found throughout Vietnam.

The indigenous people encountered by these Indian traders lived in villages and walled towns and practiced animist spirit worship. (Time-Life, 1995:15)

These were the *Cham* people of the kingdom of *Champa*.

Around the same time the Khmer empire was ruling in Angkor (Cambodia) to the west, Cham civilization thrived in central and southern Vietnam and dominated the coastal plains of Vietnam for almost 1,000 years, from the 2nd to the 15th centuries AD.

Vietnamese history is said to begin with the Cham, its oldest inhabitants.

Like the 'Yards, the Cham were originally a Malayo-Polynesian people. They dominated much of central and southern Vietnam from the 2nd to the 15th century, until finally forced out by encroaching northerners.

FYI: Small numbers of Cham still live in the Mekong area.

After the arrival of the Europeans, many 'Yards and Cham became Christian, mostly Catholic and Lutheran. Despite this, they never completely abandoned their animistic beliefs where spirit-placating ceremonies were performed by powerful shamans known as the Kings of Fire, Wind, and Water, respectively.

———

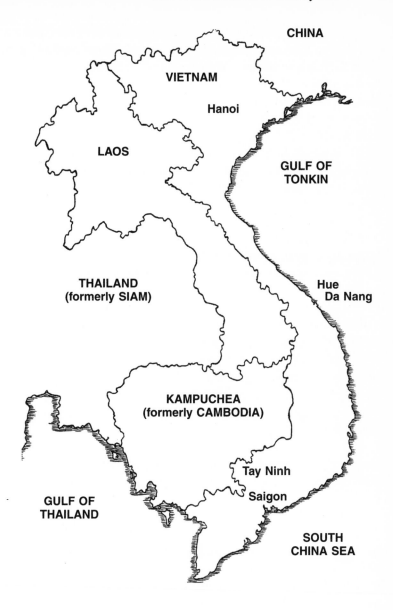

Figure 1

Map of Vietnam

Meanwhile, in the north were also "Vietnamese" whose culture was closely related to the Han-Chinese. Though related ethnically, these northern "Chinese-Vietnamese" had been at war with the Chinese of China off and on for 2,000 years.

The words "Viet Nam" literally mean "moving south," which is exactly what these northern "Chinese-Vietnamese" — who would become today's "Vietnamese" — did, displacing earlier inhabitants of the south, such as the 'Yards and the Cham.

In addition to these northern "Chinese-Vietnamese," there were indigenous peoples of the north with cultural and racial links to Siam (now called Thailand), Cambodia (now called Kampuchea), and Laos (still called Laos, last time we looked).

Down through the ages, these various peoples would continue to crowd, then openly clash, and all too often crush one another, putting aside their petty prejudices and personal ambitions only long enough to join together to combat foreign invaders: the Chinese, the French, the Japanese, the French again, and finally, the Americans.

There is an ancient Chinese adage: "Let my child live in exciting times." The reasoning being that "exciting times" lead to more opportunities in life, more chances to succeed.

If "living in exciting times" is indeed a blessing, then the land and peoples of Vietnam can truly be said to have been born under a lucky star!

Chapter Two
Phan Dau: "To Strive and to Struggle"

No matter where or when you live, life is a constant study in *Phan Dau*, striving and struggling — easier for some, harder for others.

Kiep So, "Fate," has never made life "easy" for the Vietnamese. When not busy fighting amongst themselves, they were busy repelling foreign invaders. Thus, any study of Vietnamese history is a study in striving, a lesson in struggle — a course in survival!

The same fire that crafts sword steel can all too easily consume a piece of bamboo. Yet humble bamboo will continue to bend long after the haughty steel blade has snapped a 'twain. So too it is with hardy people: They rise, they fall, they get back up again.

Thus the samurai declaration: "Nine times down, ten times up!"

Dynasties and kingdoms also rise, and fall, only to rise again in adapted, more resilient form.

Such is the nature of things. Such are the ways of men.

What follows is a short history of Vietnamese *Phan Dau*.

The Ancient of Days

800–300 BC: The *Dong Son* civilization thrives in the Red River Valley near present-day Hanoi, in northern Vietnam.

500 BC: The *Van Lang* kingdom founded by the semi-mythical Hung kings in the Black River Valley and the Red River Valley in the north.

258 BC: The kingdom of An Lac founded by An Duong.

The Coming of the Chinese

207 BC: An official of China's *Ch'in* Dynasty (221–207) named Zhao Tuo (called *Trien Da* by the Vietnamese) founds the kingdom of *Nam Viet* in North Vietnam.

124 BC: The Chinese *Han Dynasty* (207 BC–220 AD) invades northern Vietnam.

43 BC: China finally "subdues" northern Vietnam after brutally crushing a rebellion led by the legendary Trung sisters.

FYI: China will, in effect, rule Vietnam for the next 1,000 years. Not until 939 AD will Vietnam succeed in throwing off the Chinese yoke.

100 AD: Champa civilization emerges in central Vietnam.

111 AD: Tonkin and Annam conquered by China.

FYI: Words like "conquered" and "controlled" are relative terms, especially when talking about Vietnam.

The *Han*, like so many would-be conquerors of Vietnam, may have taken over a city or two and even "pacified" a small section of the countryside, but the reality remained that rebels (always called "bandits") still ruled the hills and pirates (some political, most merely out for profit) still controlled the waterways and harassed the coastline.

To quote Khan Noonian Singh: "Conquest is easy, control is not!"

Dynasty and Decay

939 AD: The Chinese are finally driven out of Vietnam by a popular revolt led by Ngo Quyen.

944: Ruler Quyen dies and for the next 500 years a series of mostly short-lived dynasties (e.g., the Ly, the Tran) rule patchwork portions of Vietnam with varying degrees of success.

1407: The Chinese Ming Dynasty (1368–1644) seizes control of northern Vietnam.

1428: Warlord Le Loi finally drives out the Ming and establishes the Le Dynasty.

Le Loi celebrates by invading the south and eventually conquering Champa.

1471: Having defeated Champa, the Annan Empire conquers southward in Cochin.

1527: The Le Dynasty is ousted by the Mac Dynasty.

1540: The Mac Dynasty is officially recognized by the Chinese Ming Dynasty.

1545: Le Dynasty loyalists regain control over central Vietnam.

1592: Le loyalist forces will continue fighting Le authority for the next 35 years.

1600: Le Dynasty forces are split after fighting breaks out between the powerful Trinh and Nguyen clans of the Le court.

From this point on, the Le imperial court rules in name only and is powerless to prevent the two rival factions from dividing the country between them.

In short order, warlords loyal to the Trinh control the northern half of the country, while Nguyen warlords rule in the south.

This kind of internecine fighting couldn't have arrived at a worse time for the Vietnamese, nor at a better time for the latest arrivals to Southeast Asia... Europeans!

The Coming of the Europeans

1254 AD: Marco Polo gets the credit for being the first European to visit Vietnam, visiting Burma and sections of Vietnam between 1254 and 1324.

1265–1331: East Indian Friar Odoric of Pordenome visits Champa.

1400s: Venetian Niccoló dei Conti is the next European to wade ashore in Southeast Asia, bringing detailed information on the region back to Europe.

1555: Portuguese and Spanish are already active in India, Siam, and Burma. Portuguese missionaries have penetrated into Cambodia.

1600: Dutch, British, and French all "invade" Southeast Asia before the end of the 16th century.

Not wanting to miss out on getting their piece of the Asian pie, in the late 1600s a "Free Enterprise" of French freebooters tried to muscle the King of Siam into making exclusive trade concessions, in effect, asking him to sign away his land to them.

After a few impromptu — and bloody! — lessons in Thai kickboxing and swordsmanship, the French freebooters beat a hasty retreat, prudently deciding to seek easier pickings, and their fortunes, elsewhere.

The French find both in Vietnam. Weakened by decades of fighting between clans and petty warlords, Vietnam was ripe for the taking. By the second half of the 19th century, the French will control all of Vietnam.

1859: French capture Saigon.

They then extend their control over all of Tonkin and Annan.

1862: French annex Cochin China, effectively making them the rulers of all Vietnam.

Ultimately, the French extend their claims west into Cambodia and Laos, which they combined as "Indochina." The French will rule this Indochinese colonial empire, including Vietnam, for the next 100 years. Recall that "rule" is a relative term!

The 20th-Century Struggle

Up to modern days, Vietnam has continued to "live in exciting times:"

1926: The Cao Dai religious sect is formally founded (See detailed account in Section II).

1939: The Hoa Hao sect, often described as "militant Buddhists," is founded.

1940: Imperial Japan takes control of Vietnam without firing a shot following the French surrender early in World War II.

1941: The Viet Minh guerrilla force is founded under the leadership of Ho Chi Minh (1890–1969) to fight the Japanese.

1943: The Cao Dai militia is established for self-defense and in order to oppose the Japanese.

1945: Japan surrenders. World War II ends.

1946: Following the Japanese withdrawal, the French attempt to reassert colonial authority over Vietnam.

1946: The Viet Minh attack the French.

1954: French forces lose 15,000 men at the 55-day siege of Dien

Bien Phu. North Vietnam falls to the Viet Minh.

At the Geneva Conference held that same year, Vietnam is officially divided into North and South pending U.N. sanctioned nationwide elections.

1955: The French officially leave Vietnam.

With U.S. blessing and backing, Premier Ngo Dinh Diem (1901–1963) declares an independent republic in the South and refuses to hold elections. America's "Vietnam War" has unofficially begun.

1956: The Communist *Viet Nam Cong San* (the "Viet Cong") guerrilla army is formed in the South to oppose Diem and "reunite" Vietnam.

1956: Diem, a staunch Catholic, orders the Cao Dai militia to disband.

1961: The U.S. signs a treaty with Diem and begins pouring massive economic and military aid into South Vietnam.

1963: Diem is killed in a coup led by Buddhist generals. Chaos reigns in the South until Nguyen Van Thieu, one of the officers who helped overthrow Diem, takes power in 1967. Thieu remains president until 1975.

1965: U.S. bombs North Vietnam. Over 500,000 U.S. troops now in Vietnam. American Vietnam War drags on, eventually spreading to Cambodia and Laos.

1973: A cease-fire is declared. American troops begin withdrawing.

1975: Saigon falls. America's "Vietnam War" ends.

1976: The unified Socialist Republic of Vietnam proclaimed. Over 100,000 Vietnamese "boat people" flee the country.

Post-1976: Cao Dai religion is repressed by the victorious Communists.

Chapter Three
Man Den: "The Black Curtain"

In his classic *Ping Fa* (*The Art of War*), Chinese Master Sun Tzu (circa 500 BC) describes two types of force: *cheng* (direct force) and *ch'i* (indirect force).

Applied to military operations, *cheng* corresponds to the traditional movements of men and material and to conventional ways of combating an enemy. *Ch'i* on the other hand refers to unconventional and indirect tactics, clandestine and guerrilla operations.

Vietnamese call these latter types of operations *Man Den*, "the Black Curtain." This heading includes any strategy and/or tactic designed to blind your foes to your true intentions.

Man Den also refers to ways of influencing affairs from behind the scene (from behind a "black curtain," get it?). In this sense, Man Den can be used as a synonym for espionage and intrigue in general.

One of the nicknames for the Cao Dai warrior is *Co den*, meaning "black flag," an obvious nod to the "black curtain" clandestine techniques they were known to employ.

FYI: Chiefs in the Japanese "Mafia," the *Yakuza*, are known as *Kuromaku*, "Black Curtains." (See "From Buddha to Black Dragons" later in this chapter.)

———

Researchers are all too often so dazzled by the "big" battles and the "major" players in history that they miss the subtleties and backroom double-dealings — the daggers in the night, the poison dropped in just the right cup, the timely whispers tickling just the right ear — those seldom spoken of schemes and skullduggeries that all too often have more to say about who wins and loses a particular battle — or who wins or loses an entire *empire!*

So it is with Vietnamese history.

While the country as a whole has been so obviously ravaged by open conflict, Vietnam has just as often fallen victim to *gian lan*, *gian tra*, actions "clandestine and crafty," intrigues as opposed to incendiaries that determine in advance the outcome of battles, while predicting the stumblings of an empire.

Throughout her history, Vietnam has been plagued by vicious court intrigues and by the diabolical double-dealings of every ilk of opportunist from the rabidly rapine to religious fanatics, from free-booters to Freemasons.

From privateers to priests, Jesuits to jackanapes, whether missionary, mercenary or a balance of both, all these rascals have in their own way — either through their success or more often than not through their abysmal failures! — contributed to Vietnamese history in general and the rise of the Cao Dai religion in particular.

These sly and subtle influences, from both East and West, inexorably twisted their cold tentacles around Vietnam's warm heart — from cultic secret societies spawned in China and Japan, to no less formidable and shadowy forces such as Freemasons from France.

Each of these groups would have their own influence on the development of Vietnam as a nation as well as on the emergence of the mysterious Cao Dai religious sect which, in turn, would itself be influential in the 20th century history of Vietnam.

The Illuminati Conspiracy

Everyone's heard of the Illuminati, that sinister cabal of powerful men who "pull the strings" of world politics and finance from behind the scenes — from behind a "black curtain!"

However much of the exaggeration by modern conspiracists, history records there really was a "sinister" secretive order called the Illuminati.

Actually, there were two such groups.

In 1776, a small group of intellectuals in Bavaria were harassed by their government for founding a "subversive" secret society known as the "Illuminati." This short-lived, largely ineffectual group had taken its inspiration and its name from a much older, much more effective, secret society also known as the Illuminati.

The original Illuminati, founded in France in the 13th century, was a consortium of "business-minded" individuals who came together secretly in Paris to finance "Free Enterprise" expeditions (i.e., "crusades") into the Middle East.

It is important to understand that, at this time, only the Pope could authorize a "Holy Crusade." Under the blessing of the Pope, European crusades were free to invade, rape and pillage "the Holy Land" so long as they gave all glory to God and a lion's share of their booty to the Vatican.

Not willing to trust their own ill-gotten gains to the lopsided Vatican scales, the founders of the Illuminati (the word means "Enlightened Ones") had decided to strike out on their own.

The need for secrecy was vital, since going against the Pope during the Middle Ages would, at the very least, get you ex-communicated — pretty much damning your soul for all eternity. Worst case scenario: Getting into a pissing contest with the Pope won you an invite to one of the Vatican's infamous barbeques . . . and you don't want to know where they stuck the shish kebab!

The original Illuminati was represented by thirteen entrepreneurs which included several prosperous merchants, bankers, the Grandmasters of various Knight Orders, the King of France, and a handful of "heretical cultists." One of these thirteen seats is said to have been reserved for the infamous Grandmaster of the Islamic Cult of the (H)assassins. (See *Assassins: Secrets of the Cult of Assassins*, by Dr. Haha Lung, Paladin Press, 1997.)

To throw Vatican bloodhounds off their scent, the Illuminati began a disinformation campaign meant to discredit the noble Order of Knights Templars (whose Grandmaster had reportedly refused one of the thirteen seats on the Illuminati's Supreme Council).

This black propaganda was so successful it led to the destruction of the Templars, allowing the Illuminati to seize the Templars' considerable assets.

FYI: Ironically, one of the many false charges the Illuminati leveled against the Templars (in addition to Satanism, sodomy, and sundry loiterings!) was that the Templars had made secret treaties with the dreaded Order of (H)assassins in Syria. A charge the Illuminati were themselves guilty of. (Ibid.)

———

With the help of Robert the Bruce of Scotland, those Templars surviving the Vatican-sponsored massacre founded the Order of Scottish Rite Masons, what we today know as "Freemasons" . . . which the Illuminati quickly infiltrated and turned to their own purposes!

French Freemasons

Down through the ages there have been numerous offshoots and imitators of the original Templar/Scottish Rite Freemasons. Imitation really is the greatest form of flattery.

Unfortunately, there is often a thin line between fame and infamy.

Down through the ages, Freemasons have also been accused of starting every war, of having created slavery, and of releasing various plagues and diseases on mankind, all in order to fulfill some nebulous "master plan" for world domination as dictated by their hidden masters, the original Illuminati — still alive and kicking behind that ominous black curtain!

———

Beyond such wild allegations, what is a matter of open knowledge is that several of the Founding Fathers of the American Revolution, including George Washington, were Freemasons.

Coincidentally, the Bavarian Illuminati was founded in 1776, the same year as the founding of the United States of America.

It is also no secret that Freemasons were instrumental in helping form and ferment the French Revolution. In fact, the Comte de Mirabeau, one of the main architects of the French Revolution was a Freemason, a man who had also reportedly been initiated into the short-lived Bavarian Illuminati. (Vankin, 1992)

Throughout France's colonial history, powerful bankers and politicians belonging to various lodges of French Freemasonry were at the forefront in pushing to expand France's overseas colonial empire.

For example, it was just such backers bankrolling the freebooters who tried to extort the King of Siam into signing exclusive trading contracts with France in the late 1600s.

When that venture failed, this particular "Free Enterprise" turned its attention to Vietnam.

The All-Seeing Eye

The secret recognition symbol of the 13th century Illuminati was an All-Seeing Eye inside a delta triangle. "Delta," depicted as a triangle, is the fourth letter of the Greek alphabet, as well as the mathematical symbol for "change" and "transition."

This All-Seeing Eye within the triangle has its origins in the ancient Egyptian "Eye of Horus," a symbol of the sun, hence "Enlightenment."

FYI: Yes, this is the same symbol that today adorns the U.S. dollar bill, put there during the administration of Franklin Delano Roosevelt, at the insistence of Vice President Henry Wallace. Both Wallace and FDR were Freemasons, as were Presidents Reagan, Ford, Truman, Harding, Taft, Teddy Roosevelt, Garfield, Andrew Johnson, Buchanan, Polk, Andrew Jackson, Monroe, and the aforementioned George Washington. (Ibid.)

———

In his 1977 book, *Cosmic Trigger: The Final Secret of the Illuminati*, author Robert Anton Wilson points out that variations of this Illuminati symbol have been used by Crowley's *Ordo Templi Orientis*, on the great seal of the United States, and on documents, monuments, and lodges of Freemasons. Says Wilson, "Other forms are used by *Vietnamese Buddhists*, Theosophites, Rosicrucians, etc." (emphasis added).

Both the "mystical schools" of the Rosicrucians (founded 15th century) and Theosophy (founded 1875) can be traced back to Freemasonry, hence to the Illuminati.

By "Vietnamese Buddhists," Wilson means the Cao Dai, often erroneously identified as a "sect" of Buddhism.

Illuminati referred to the All-Seeing Eye symbol as the "Shining Delta," a euphemism sometimes used in place of "Illuminati."

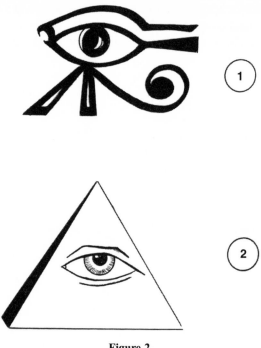

Figure 2
The All-Seeing Eye

(1) The Egyptian Eye of Horus
(2) The All-Seeing Eye, *Illuminati* emblem adapted by the Cao Dai.

In the 20th century, with the creation of the Cao Dai religion, this "Shining Delta" symbol would come to fly over another shining delta, South Vietnam's Mekong Delta.

Most of us do not have an "All-Seeing Eye," so it is impossible to say which colonial Europeans "invading" Vietnam were motivated by personal greed and glory and which were acting on orders from the collective greed of "unseen forces."

That colonial France "conquered" Vietnam in short order is a matter of historical fact.

But, as already mentioned, open battles are easy to record. All we need do is follow the noise and count the bodies.

What isn't as easily seen are the many intrigues and hidden agendas playing out behind the black curtain, masterful schemes and intricate skullduggery just as important to the unfolding of history as are bullets and bayonets.

Unfortunately, all we inevitably end up with when trying to decipher the comings and goings of crafty cabals, secret societies, and shadowy government agencies is always the same: a dancing tendril of smoke glimpsed behind us in a dark mirror, whispers, and winks.

As we shall see in Section II of this study, an inordinate amount of Illuminati/Freemasonry symbolism (re)appeared, and remains to this day, an intricate part of the inner teachings of the Cao Dai religion. Indeed, several well-known Western Freemasons are actually "worshipped" as "saints" in the Cao Dai religion!

———

"There is a visible labor and there is an invisible labor."
(Victor Hugo, author, Freemason, Cao Dai saint)

The Crowley Connection

Ever notice how curious connections and coincidences always appear when discussing secret societies?

For example, in the 1890s infamous British occultist Aleister Crowley, one time member of the secret society known as the Golden Dawn (HQ in Paris, birthplace of the original Illuminati), founded a secret society of his own known as the *Ordo Templi Orienti* (literally, "Temple of the Orient").

Crowley's O.T.O. was formed from two earlier mystical fraternities: the Hermetic Brotherhood of Light and the remnants of the defunct Bavarian Illuminati. (Wilson, 1977:96)

Crowley's O.T.O. took as its emblem the All-Seeing Eye, the same symbol later adopted by the Cao Dai.

Speaking of Vietnam and Crowley in the same breath: In January, 1906, Crowley traveled east to what he referred to as "the wilds of China." In March, 1906, he was spotted in Tonkin where, according to Crowley's own account, he fought off a band of "river pirates."

Crowley then visited Hanoi before departing for Hong Kong. (Smith, 2000:168)

During World War II, Crowley, along with such notables as authors Aldous Huxley and Ian Fleming (creator of James Bond), worked for a department of MI-6 British Intelligence called "the Occult Bureau," a think-tank given the job of deciphering and, when possible, manipulating Hitler's reliance on information drawn from "occult sources," i.e., astrology, numerology, etc.

At one point, Crowley was called in to debrief major Nazi defector Rudolf Hess. Crowley and Hess had known each other before the war.

Hess (as well as other high-ranking Nazis) had belonged to *Thulegesellschaft* (the Thule Society) and the *Vril*, German secret societies with ties to Crowley's O.T.O.

The Thule and the Vril were spin-offs from Guido von List's *Armanen*. Hitler's two main mentors, Dietrich Eckart and Karl Haushofer were members of the Armanen and it was they who convinced Hitler to adopt the Eastern swastika (Armanen's emblem) as the official emblem of the young Nazi party.

Haushofer had forged ties with several Asian occult groups and secret societies in China, Tibet, and Japan. It is reported that at one point Haushofer had occultists from the Tibetan *Green Dragon Society* flown to Berlin to perform "cleansing rites" designed to erase "Jewish influence." This "wild tale" is supported by the discovery of the bodies of several "curiously dressed Asians" (all wearing gloves) discovered in the ruins of bombed out Berlin. Whether actually Green Dragons from China and Tibet or possible members of Hitler's Japanese allies and infamous *Black Dragons*, we will probably never know.

What we do know for certain is that, beginning in the 1600s, numerous Western secret societies, fanatical religious cultists, and just as secretive political and financial groups had a major influence on the colonization and eventually subjugation of southeast Asia in general and Vietnam in particular... but no more of an influence than those equally ruthless secret societies launched *from the East!*

"Some things are secret because they are hard to know, and some because they are not fit to utter." (Francis Bacon, author, Freemason)

The Ninja Connection

When we think of "ninja" we inevitably conjure up an image of black-masked, samurai-sword-swinging assassins lurking in the shadows of medieval Japan.

But this is much too narrow a definition.

"Ninja" were not — are not! — just confined to medieval Japan, since the true definition of "ninja" includes anyone who uses secrecy and stealth in their activities. (Lung, 1997 B:12)

An expanded — more definitive — listing of "ninja" worldwide must include:

• Many diverse, *realism-intensive* martial arts schools
• Various espionage and counterespionage special operations groups (both governmental and private)
• Many accomplished combat cadres

By not limiting our definition and understanding of who and what exactly is a "ninja," we open our minds to new and more diverse training methods, tricks and techniques, any one of which, or all of which, holds the potential of making us more efficient in our own "ninja" craft.

Under our expanded definition of "ninja" we must include the ancient *Moshuh Nanren* spies of Imperial China, from whom many of the tactics and techniques employed by medieval Japanese *shinobi* ninja were derived.

We can also include on our "ninja" list the dreaded *Kali*-worshipping *Thuggee* cult of India (see: Lung, 1995), as well as the medieval Middle Eastern dagger-wielding *Hashishin*, "Assassins" (See: Lung, 1997A).

In addition, *modern* killer cadres such as Russian *Spetsnaz*, U.S. Navy SEALS, and United States Special Forces ("Green Berets") will also have to be included in this new, expanded definition of "ninja." (Lung, 1998)

Unfortunately, our expanded definition will also have to include many of the most treacherous terrorist groups operating in the world. In fact, any accomplished hit man, burglar, or other felon whose respective criminal craft requires they employ stealth and skullduggery will have to be placed on our "ninja" alumni list. (Lung, 1997 B:12)

Under this expanded — more accurate — definition, it is not hard to see how Vietnamese fighters in general, and *Cao Dai* warriors in particular, qualify as "ninja." This "ninja connection" becomes all the more obvious when we take time to examine the roots and direct influences other "ninja" cadres, from Chinese "forest demons" to Japanese secret societies, played on the development of Vietnamese martial arts.

Moshuh Nanren, Chinese "Ninja"

"By its very nature any history of the Shinobiman must be incomplete. For the Ninja, secrecy was/is power." (Lung, 1997 B:23)

It is no secret early Japanese culture was influenced by Chinese culture, as was the culture of Vietnam.

What isn't as well known is that the origins of the (in)famous Japanese ninja can also be traced directly back to Mainland China.

China possesses a long and bloody tradition of spies and assassins. Chinese military genius Sun Tzu (500 BC) devoted a whole chapter in his masterpiece *The Art of War* to the use of "secret agents." The vastness of the Chinese realm demanded that any Emperor who wanted to remain in power had better maintain an effective network of espionage and counterespionage operatives.

The best known of these killer cadres were the *Moshuh Nanren*.

The Moshuh Nanren were part state police, part secret society, entrusted with maintaining the safety of the Emperor and his dynasty.

The Moshuh Nanren were already active in China prior to the first century AD.

These Moshuh Nanren operated as part Gestapo, part Special Forces, assigned to root out, swiftly swoop down on, and then mercilessly crush any real or imagined threats to the Emperor. Moshuh Nanren instantly and efficiently quelled any potential dissent and disruption by literally cutting off the head of any reform "movement," subversive secret society, or open rebellion against Imperial edict.

Like today's state-sanctioned "death squads," terror was the Moshuh Nanren's most effective weapon.

As the ancient Chinese adage advises: "Kill one to control ten thousand."

Like the Japanese ninja who followed in their footsteps, Moshuh Nanren deliberately cultivated their victims' fear by encouraging the superstition their agents were descended from mythical *Lin Kuei*, "forest demons," just as Japanese ninja would later cultivate the propaganda they were descended from the Japanese Storm God *Susano* by way of half-man/half-crow forest demons known as *Tengu*.

Imperially sanctioned Moshuh Nanren existed in one form or another for several centuries, faithfully serving the Chinese Imperial court.

However, whenever a new dynasty took the throne, the new Emperor/bloodline would immediately purge the ministers, spies, assassins, and executioners of their predecessor suspected of questionable loyalty.

When this happened, some dedicated Moshuh Nanren committed the Chinese equivalent of *Hari Kiri*, following their beloved master into The Void, rather than serve the new Emperor.

Other Moshuh Nanren ran like Hell!

Still other Moshuh Nanren, whose respective Emperors had met with foul play, went underground, vowing vengeance on those who had usurped power from their master.

As a result, down through the centuries, the tactics and techniques of these displaced Moshuh Nanren slowly filtered out to other elements of Chinese society.

Some disenfranchised Moshuh Nanren founded secret societies (ironically similar to those they had originally been sanctioned to root out and destroy while working for the Emperor). These Moshuh Nanren secret societies then carried out subversive political and criminal activities against the new dynasty.

Still other Moshuh Nanren simply became criminals, either hiring their stealth skills out to the highest bidder, or else simply using those skills to line their own pockets.

Fortunately for us, some of the best fighting (i.e., killing) techniques of the Moshuh Nanren were eventually incorporated into mainstream Chinese *wu shu* (martial arts).

It is not surprising that techniques originally developed by Moshuh Nanren are credited with influencing other martial arts and inspiring guerrilla and criminal cadres from the *hwarangdo* warriors of Korea to the Cao Dai warriors of Vietnam.

Of course, the Moshuh Nanren's best known imitators were the shinobi ninja of Japan.

From Buddha to Black Dragons

Between the first and fifth centuries AD, Moshuh Nanren tactics and techniques infiltrated into Japan. However, the actual word "ninja" did not come into popular use until the Shotoku War of succession in the sixth century when Japanese prince Shotoku went to war with the Moriya clan over who would be Emperor.

Shotoku was fighting a losing battle until he began taking the advice of a freebooter named Otomo-No-Saijin. Otomo's *nom de guerre* was "Shinobi," which means "The one who sneaks in." In other words, a "ninja."

FYI: The word "ninja" comes from the Japanese *kanji*-writing for "shinobi," the first strokes of which mean "spirit," the second part of which means "edge."

Where this mysterious Otomo had garnered his "ninja" skills isn't known for certain, although it doesn't take a great leap of the imagination to figure that Otomo may have acquired skills originating with the Moshuh Nanren.

Some experts have gone so far as to speculate that Otomo might himself have been a Moshuh Nanren spy and *agent provocateur* for the Chinese Imperial Court determined to influence Japanese politics.

If true, this would not be the first, nor hardly the last time, China would send spies into Japan and neighboring countries.

Shotoku was a Buddhist. Following his victory over the Moriya, his patronage allowed Buddhist monasteries to prosper in Japan.

Buddhism was first brought to Japan in 586 AD, at the time of the Yamato Imperial court. The Yamato Emperor was so taken with Buddhism that he sent several students to China to study the religion.

Moshuh Nanren spy-masters took advantage of this opportunity to both "convert" (i.e., subvert) some of these young visitors into becoming spies while, simultaneously, infiltrating many of their own agents into the ranks of Buddhist Masters and monks invited to Japan to teach.

Down through the years, many of these spies helped found and/or infiltrated Japanese Buddhist monasteries, as well as the temples of the indigenous Japanese religion of *Shinto*, and the enclaves of a popular folk religion (combining Buddhism, Shinto, and Animism) known as *Shugendo*.

Many of these monasteries, temples, and enclaves were built in mountainous regions. The monks of these literal fortresses were known as *Yamabushi*, literally "Mountain warriors," since many of them were *Ronin* (masterless) samurai who spent more time learning martial arts than they did reading scripture.

By the beginning of the Heian Period (794–1194 AD), Buddhism had firmly established itself as a religious force to be reckoned with.

Yamabushi monasteries grew so powerful so fast, some were able to field hundreds of heavily armed warrior-monks. In addition, in times of threat, many of these diverse orders of monks would band together for mutual protection. Needless to say, local *daimyo* (samurai lords) soon began to fear these mountain warriors.

By the 12th century, Japanese officials had had enough and began systematically destroying these various strongholds, resulting in the death and dispersion of several of these Yamabushi orders.

Many of those Yamabushi surviving this purge settled in Iga and Koga provinces in central Japan where they became farmers.

Farmers by day, *ninja* by night!

Some of these "farmers" began hiring their considerable martial arts skills out to the highest bidder, easily playing one samurai faction off against the other.

From the 12th century up through the 16th century, great "shi-nobi ninja" clans, as many as 50 by some counts, ruled a virtually autonomous kingdom in central Japan.

When samurai did dare venture into this area, they did so heavily armed and in force and then found only disappointment and death from behind!

This situation can be likened to the frustrations American troops encountered when trying to roust an entrenched cadre of Viet Cong from a particular area.

In both instances, "invaders" met stiff resistance in the form of shadows who stubbornly refused to hold still long enough to be shot, and from wisps of smoke that suddenly materialized behind you, shot you full of holes, and then just as quickly disappeared!

Shinobi ninja struck fear into the hearts of civilians and samurai alike well up into the 16th century.

But all good things must end. While the savage internecine war-fare between various samurai factions was the bread and butter of the shinobi ninja, the unification of Japan under Hideyoshi Toyotomi in 1590 spelled doom for the great clans.

FYI: Ironically, Hideyoshi — the only commoner to hold power in Japan — started his rise to power as a "ninja" thief and high-wayman, before graduating to being a spy, and eventually a lieu-tenant to warlord Oda Nobunga.

After Nobunga died, Hideyoshi made short work of his rivals and then went to work on the shinobi. Hideyoshi's ruthlessness and suc-cessful efforts at unification quickly put an end to the great shinobi clans.

Reading the writing on the wall, the more adept of these shinobi prudently decided to go into other lines of work. Other ninja groups turned to crime, eventually joining the ranks of *Yakuza* gangsters. Still other clans, such as the Hattori, noted for their bodyguarding skills, helped create the modern Japanese police.

By the beginning of the 20th century, you had Yakuza gangsters — descended from ninja — playing cat and mouse with police — also descended from ninja!

Still other ninja helped swell the ranks of the numerous nationalist secret societies that began popping up after Commodore Perry forced Japan to open her ports to trade in 1854.

These secret societies enlisted ninja-trained agents to carry out spying and assassinations inside Japan as well as overseas.

Some of these secret societies were closely allied with — and bankrolled by — the powerful samurai families controlling Japan's military-industrial complex known as the *zaibatsu*.

In turn, the zaibatsu were closely allied with the military and thus with the military's intelligence bureau, the much-feared *Kempeitai*.

Kempeitai operatives were "ninja" in the traditional sense of the word, carrying out intelligence gathering, assassination, and general skullduggery wherever Japanese interests were involved.

So closely intertwined were these nationalist secret societies and cliques that it is impossible to say where one left off and the other began. In fact, one man might belong to several different, yet inter-connected, groups. For example, a rich Yakuza "businessman" might belong to the same nationalist secret society as the police detective assigned to investigate him. These two would, in turn, hobnob with a general in the military, or a member of the Kempeitai — all united by their nationalism.

These groups sent spies overseas for various reasons:

* The military to spy out rival military threat potentials
* Agents working for a zaibatsu concern sent to infiltrate companies overseas in order to keep a leg up on the competition
* Numerous secret societies infiltrating student unions and martial arts clubs, both inside Japan, and abroad

The most effective of these secret societies were the Black Ocean Society (founded 1881) and the Black Dragon Society (founded 1901).

The Black Ocean Society (*Genyosha*) was founded by wealthy samurai-turned-businessman, Kotaro Hiraoka.

Originally confined to Kyushu province in Japan, the Black Ocean Society was soon fielding agents and recruiting turncoats overseas to spy and exert influence on China, Korea, Manchuria, Russia and Indochina, including Vietnam. (Lung, 1997 B:40)

The Black Ocean was the consummate school for spies — gathering intelligence and mastering manipulation, as well as an international terrorist organization, in many ways foreshadowing today's Al Qaeda terrorist network.

Black Ocean operatives infiltrated religious organizations, student unions, and already-existing secret societies both inside Japan and abroad.

The Black Ocean was especially active gathering information and extending its influence into Manchuria, where founder Kotaro Hiraoka owned large tracts of mining land.

So successful was the Black Ocean Society that it spawned numerous imitators and offshoots.

The most (in)famous offshoot of the Black Ocean Society was the Black Dragon Society.

The Black Dragon Society (Japanese *Kokurkykai*), also known as the Amur Society, was founded in 1901 in order to carry out intelligence-gathering and terrorism operations in Korea and China.

The Black Dragon was formed after evidence surfaced implicating Black Ocean "ninja" in the assassination of Queen Min of Korea in 1895.

Founded by Kotaro Hiraoka's disciple Rychei Uchida, the Black Dragon's stated purpose was to push the Russians out of Manchuria, back across the Amur River, which forms the northern border of Manchuria.

The Black Dragon Society grew at a phenomenal rate and, in short order, had taken over most operations of the Black Ocean to become the most powerful secret society of Japan.

Some Black Dragon supporters were openly known, but the vast majority of its members remained undercover.

Unlike the Black Ocean, who had had few qualms about enlisting known criminals and killers into its ranks, the Black Dragon concentrated on recruiting "clean slate" students into its ranks, students who could be trained (i.e., "molded"), students eager to become *Soshi* (Japanese "Brave Knights") of the Black Dragon.

The true leaders of Japan, the rich samurai (zaibatsu) families who ran the military-industrial complex, soon learned the value of having "ninja" in the right place at the right time.

During the Russo-Japanese War (1904–05), Black Dragon "ninja" obtained detailed plans of the Russian naval installation at Port Arthur (Lu-shun, China), allowing the Japanese to stage a surprise attack and sink the Russian fleet.

FYI: Forty years later, the Japanese would use this same tried-and-true "ninja" strategy at a place called Pearl Harbor!

Following their victory over the Russians, Japanese leaders openly fed the Black Dragon (and similar nationalist secret societies) by pouring money and manpower into their overseas espionage operations. As a result, Black Dragon cells were soon operating worldwide, from Hong Kong to the United States, and from Manchuria to Indochina.

At its height in 1944, the Black Dragon would boast over 10,000 members!

By the 1930s evidence of Black Dragon influence and subterfuge could be found as far away as the United States, throughout the Caribbean, in Ethiopian Africa and Turkey.

Prior to WWII, the Black Dragon went out of its way to establish alliances with nationalist and fascist subversive groups worldwide, including the White Wolf Society of Turkey and the Hung Brothers of China. In anticipation of the Axis alliance, the Black Dragon formed dark pacts with several occult-oriented secret societies in Germany including the Thule Society and the Vril, whose membership included several prominent Nazis.

Closer to home in Asia, Black Dragon operatives continued infiltrating religious groups, secret societies, and fringe political groups, from Singapore to Hong Kong, to Peking.

One version of history has the Black Dragons supporting Sun-Yat-Sen as China's first president. Another version has the Black Dragons responsible for his untimely death in 1925 — a death which helped plunge China into a decades-long civil war, further weakening an already divided China, making her easy pickings for the coming Japanese invasion.

Through infiltration of Chinese secret societies, the Black Dragon was able to establish a "fifth column" of secret supporters and subversives inside the British colony of Hong Kong in anticipation of Japan seizing the colony during WWII.

Likewise, Black Dragon operatives infiltrated key organizations — governmental posts, religious groups, disaffected political fringe groups, and secret societies — in dozens of other Asian countries, including Vietnam.

As in other parts of the world in general and Asia in particular, Black Dragon operatives burrowed their way into dozens of key organizations in Vietnam in anticipation of their wrenching control of colonial Indochina from the French during WWII.

Not only did Japanese agents infiltrate already existing Vietnamese *hôi kin* (secret societies) but, where expedient, Japanese agents actually *founded* and funded several Vietnamese secret societies and religious fringe groups, many of which would later prove influential in the development of Vietnamese politics in general and the rise of the Cao Dai sect in particular.

Section II
Cao Dai: "The High Tower"

In addition to all the obvious foreign political influences on her history, down through the centuries many less obvious, less well-known *religious forces* have had a major influence on the development of Vietnamese culture in general, and on its religious schools of thought in particular, culminating in the 20th century emergence of the Cao Dai.

Early on, its unique location put Vietnam directly along the route merchants, missionaries and pilgrims — Hindu Brahmans and Buddhists — traveled between India and China.

Thus the first of many foreign religious influences to land in Vietnam was Hinduism from India.

Hinduism has a diverse variety of beliefs and practices ranging from the mainstream worship of major Hindu gods such as Shiva the Destroyer, to more mystical *tantric* practices involving everything from ritual sex to sèances designed to communicate with the dead.

Early Vietnam was heavily influenced by Hinduism, as evidenced by the fact that *linga* (phallic monuments) to Shiva can be found throughout southern Vietnam.

However, even before the arrival of Indian religious influences, Vietnamese people already had an elaborate system of beliefs and practices, collectively known as "animism."

Despite invasion by numerous foreign religious traditions, many of the beliefs and practices of this indigenous animism have continued down through to the 20th century and the founding of the Cao Dai.

Chapter Four
Yeu Ma: Spirits and Saints

Anthropologists believe animism was early man's *original* expression of religion. Animists believe everything is alive, that all things have a spirit and an awareness. This is not just limited to animate objects, such as human beings and animals. Rivers, mountains, certain sacred sites — curious rock formations, groves, and grottos — all possess a conscious spirit.

This belief in all things possessing a spirit leads to two main practices in animism: First, respect for nature — since you wouldn't want to inadvertently piss off a powerful nature spirit. Second, animists communicate with these numerous spirits — honoring and petitioning peaceful and helpful spirits, while performing blood sacrifices to placate wrathful spirits.

Animism is the kind of religion practiced by Native Americans, and by the peoples of Northern Europe and Africa before the coming of Christianity and Islam.

Animism was also the original religion of Vietnam.

Animism in Vietnam

Animists in Vietnam developed an elaborate magical system (*bi hoc*) designed to keep the spirit world at bay. These include the use of *an-phu*, talismans designed to ward off evil, *phu bao*, mystical incantations, diverse divination methods, and even *xay co*, necromancy designed to communicate with (i.e., manipulate) the spirits of the dead.

The Vietnamese word *via* means both "spirit" and "vigor" and, as we will see later, is in many ways comparable to the Chinese Taoist concept of *Chi*.

According to the Vietnamese, the *via*-spirit of a person, place, or thing can be either "light" or "heavy," good or bad respectively.

In addition, there are two categories of "heavy" or malevolent spirits: *Gui* (Chinese *Kuei*), generally wrathful spirits (often associated with "haunting" specific sites), and *Ma*, the souls of the dead.

Unhappy *Ma* were much feared and were also known as *Co Hon*, literally "forsaken spirits," similar to the Buddhist concept of *pretas*, "hungry ghosts."

Elaborate rituals were developed to both placate and petition these souls of the dead.

Ancestor Worship

In his *Principles of Sociology* (1877), Herbert Spencer declared that the worship of our ancestors is at the root of every religion.

In Vietnamese animist societies, as in most animist societies, deceased ancestors (Vietnamese *Than*, Chinese *Shen*) have the power to grant boons or allay misfortune from beyond the grave. These dead ancestors possess mystical powers and can continue to influence family and community even after death. Sometimes deceased notables can ascend to the status of a god.

FYI: This is not as "bizarre" a belief as Westerners might at first imagine.

In the Japanese *Shinto* religion, the *kami* spirits of notable individuals (e.g., an honored patriarch of a powerful samurai clan, a great military leader, or an honored teacher) can become a deity. This was also the practice in pre-Christian Rome.

Even in the modern day, pious Catholics can become saints, the next best thing to being a god. Likewise, in *Mahayana* Buddhism, individuals are *encouraged* to become *Bodhisattva*, "saints" who postpone their own entrance into paradise in order to help others obtain freedom from illusion.

Vietnamese ancestor worship absorbed many of the ancestor-honoring rites so important to Confucianism. It also shared Taoism's reverence for "the Ancient Ones," past Master "Immortals" who had — through Taoist alchemy — become gods.

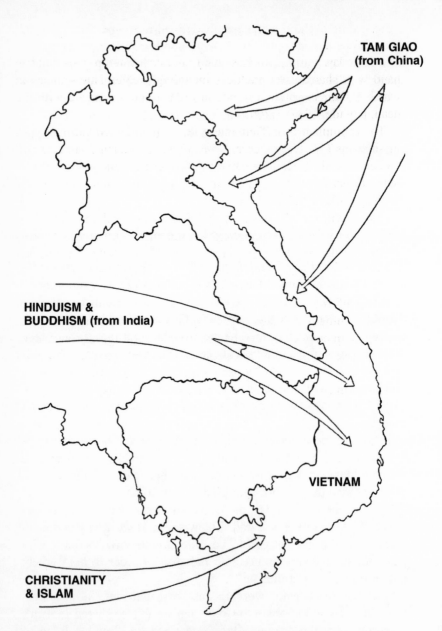

Figure 3
Religious/cultural influx into Vietnam

From Shamans to Séances

Still today, throughout East Asia ancestor worship goes hand in hand with shamanistic practices including mediumistic sèances in which a shaman enters a trance in order to communicate with the dead. (Eliade, 1987, 1:266)

To accomplish this, Vietnamese animists ordained various types of shamans (*Thay*, "sorcerers," *phu thuy*, "magicians," and *ba cot*, "witches"), all specialists capable of entering trance-like states at will in order to communicate both with spirits of nature and with the restless souls of the dead.

As we will see, the entrenched belief in the wisdom of the dead and in the validity of sèances as a means to communicate with saintly spirits would play a major role in the founding of Cao Dai.

———

Most of the duties of these indigenous Vietnamese shamans would eventually be taken over by Buddhist priests. But rather than being completely destroyed by these Chinese religious "invaders," Vietnamese animism and ancestor worship was actually reinforced by the arrival of Confucianism (with its emphasis on filial piety) and Taoism (with its reverence for nature and spirits).

Chapter Five
Tam Giao: The Three Ways

It's no secret Vietnamese culture was strongly influenced by the three organized religious traditions coming from China: Confucianism, Taoism, and Buddhism, known to the Chinese as *San-chiao*, "the Three Teachings."

Called *Tam Giao*, "the Three Ways," by the Vietnamese, these three religions, collectively and individually, directly influenced the direction of Vietnamese religion — and Southeast Asian politics — in general, and the development of the Cao Dai in particular.

Each of these three religions added a unique dash of spice to Vietnam's already complex religious stew.

But rather than being overshadowed by these new arrivals, Vietnamese animism and ancestor worship was actually reinforced by "the Three Ways" imported from China, with Buddhist priests assuming many of the duties traditionally performed by shamans, while both Taoism and Confucianism contributed to the Vietnamese belief in ancestor worship.

As we shall see, both ancient shamanism and belief in communication with the dead would play major roles in the rituals of the 20th century Cao Dai.

Khung Giao: Confucianism

Though credited with creating one of the major "religions" of the world, Kung-fu-tzu (551-479 BC), called Confucius by Westerners, didn't directly address himself to the existence of God. Rather, his masterwork *Analects* champions an ethical system call *K'ung-chiao*, a "guide to right living," a social philosophy teaching a code of con-

Tam Giao: The Triple Teachings (Chinese *San-Chiao*)

English	Vietnamese	Chinese	Founder
Taoism (aka Dao lao)	Lao giao	Tao-chiao China	Lao Tzu 500 BCE,
Confuciansim	Khong giao	K'ung-chiao	Confucius 500 BCE, China
Buddhism	Phat giao	Fo-chiao	Siddhartha Gautama 500 BCE, North India

Additional Religious Influences:

Native animism (spirit worship)
Ancestor worship

Catholicism (Vietnamese *Dao Thien Chu'a*)
Protestantism (Vietnamese *Tian giao*)

Figure 4

Tam Giao: *Religious influences on the development of the Cao Dai*

duct based on the high moral principles of peacefulness, humanity, wisdom, and courage.

Above all, Confucius stressed the obedience of children to their parents, and subjects to their rulers.

The end result of following this path was order and harmony between the three divisions of reality: Heaven, Earth, and Man: "Peaceful individuals make peaceful families. Peaceful families make peaceful villages. Peaceful villages make peaceful kingdoms. Peaceful kingdoms create a peaceful world."

Confucius' emphasis on the fidelity of children to parents was an ethic already dear to the Vietnamese, and only helped reinforce their belief in honoring ancestors — even beyond the grave.

Likewise, Confucianism's insistence that individuals faithfully serve superiors — students to teachers, subjects serving the state — helped form the *Hung hoai* code of the Cao Dai warrior. (See "The Nine Virtues of Valiant Men," Section III.)

Lao Giao: Taoism

"He who conquers others is strong. He who conquers himself is mighty." (*Tao-te Ching*)

Lao Tzu was a contemporary of Confucius. There is even an account of a contentious meeting between these two giants of Chinese philosophy.

Having reluctantly confined his philosophy into the 81 chapters of his *Tao-te Ching*, Lao Tzu headed "West" and was never seen again . . . unless you put stock in the legend that says he later turned up in Northern India where he became mentor to young Prince Siddhartha Guatama, who would, in turn, become the Buddha.

Lao Tzu, "the Old Dragon," advocated a contemplative life in accord with nature and shunned over-intellectualizing, long-winded philosophers (such as Confucius).

According to Lao Tzu, by following "the Way of Heaven" (Chinese *Tao-chiao*) one obtained insight and immortality (some Taoist Masters are documented to have lived hundreds of years!).

We follow "the Way of Heaven" by bringing ourselves *back* into harmony with *the Tao*:

"To the Taoist, the Tao is the source from whence all things derive and unto which all things ultimately return. Tao is everything and nothing. To call it *God* in the Western sense of the word would be to limit it . . . Tao is the totality of all existence, as well as the absence of all things. In many ways it is analogous to the Buddhist concept of the Void (*sunyata*). The Tao that can be defined, confined, spoken of, or grasped with hand or mind, is not the true Tao." (Lung, 1997 B:71)

Taoism's reverence for nature went hand-in-glove with Vietnamese animism.

Later, around 520 AD, the 29th Indian Buddhist Patriarch *Bodhidharma* (called *Da-mo* by the Chinese and *Daruma* by the Japanese) established the *Ch'an* sect of Buddhism at the (in)famous *Shao-Lin* monastery in Hunan Province, China.

FYI: The legendary Bodhidharma is also credited with bringing martial arts from India to China.

Ch'an was called *Zen* in Japan where it was embraced by the samurai warriors and helped inspire their already formidable *budo-jutsu* martial arts.

In Vietnam, *Ch'an/Zen* is known as *Thien* and helped craft the creed of the Cao Dai warriors. (See *"Long Nhan:* The Way of the Cao Dai Warrior.")

Phat Giao: Buddhism

Prior to 1975, if you asked an educated Vietnamese their religion, they generally answered that they were Buddhist. (Eliade, 1987, Vol. 15:257)

As early as the first centuries CE Indian Buddhist monks were active in spreading Buddhist doctrine throughout Vietnam. Buddhist images and monastery foundations dating from the 9th century have been found in Vietnam. This testifies to the last influence Buddhism has had on Vietnam.

This influence — both religious and political — would continue up through the 20th century, stimulating both the Cao Dai and their "militant" Buddhist "rivals" the *Hoa Hao.* (See "Buddhists From Hell" later in this section.)

The impact of Buddhism on Vietnamese history cannot be under-estimated:

"Vietnam has been largely excluded from the story of the development of the classical Buddhist Southeast Asian states because of the predominance of Hinduism [in] early Vietnamese history and the overwhelming cultural influence of China on the country. Until the 11th century the Vietnamese were effectively a group within the Chinese empire, and they looked to China for cultural inspiration even after they achieved independence under the Ly dynasty (1009-1224). Mahayana Buddhism was certainly part of the Chinese cultural influence and the Ch'an (Vietnamese *Thien*) school, allegedly first established in 580 CE ... was the major Buddhist tradition in Vietnam. The elite eventually came to prefer Confucianism, but Buddhism continued to be important among the masses." (Ibid. 15:395)

The type of Buddhism prevalent among the masses in Vietnam was "folk Buddhism," Buddhism mixed with indigenous animist beliefs.

Folk Buddhism

The immediate goal of Buddhism is to relieve suffering *in this world*. Therefore, orthodox Buddhism lacks dogma and adopts and adapts whatever is necessary to get its message across.

Buddhist teachers in Vietnam were thus free to mix traditional Buddhist scriptures with the magical and mystical beliefs of common folk, as well as to incorporate local "elementals," spirits and gods, and to use accepted ritual techniques (incantations, charms, etc.) familiar to the average Vietnamese because of their widespread use by tribal and village shamans.

Thus, in Vietnam as elsewhere, Buddhist priests were (still are) often found performing many of the rituals once performed by local shamans.

The Vietnamese version of "folk Buddhism" thus used many of the same indigenous symbols, beliefs, and practices as native shamans, changing these time-honored symbols and rituals very little, the result being that Buddhism in Vietnam now included a wide range of "supernatural" practices and beings.

Folk Buddhism in Vietnam also included widespread belief in benevolent and malevolent supernatural "powers" that were either to be avoided at all costs, or else deliberately sought out in order to petition their aid. These "powers" ranged from gods borrowed from the Hindu pantheon, to animistic nature spirits, and the restless ghosts of deceased ancestors. (See *Shadow Power! Secrets of the Ninja Shaman*, by Dr. Haha Lung, publication pending 2002.)

This transition from animism to folk Buddhism was made all the easier since many of the "supernormal powers" exhibited by Buddhist meditation masters were identified in the minds of Vietnamese animists with the mystical powers exhibited by their own shamans.

Each of the Tam Giao "Three Ways" contributed in its own way to the development of Vietnamese religion.

Unlike the religious factions in Europe and the Middle East, religions in Vietnam seldom clashed.

In Vietnam, as elsewhere in the Far East, Confucianism, Taoism, and Buddhism "blended" with one another, borrowing freely from one another, until it became almost impossible to distinguish where one left off and the other began:

"It goes without saying that, as in China, each of the elements composing the Triple Religion in no way presented itself as impervious to the other two. Mutual borrowings throughout the course of centuries increased to the point that it was sometimes difficult to know with certainty which rite or belief to attribute to which element." (Ibid. 5:375)

If the Tam Giao had been the *only* three "foreign" religions to "visit" Vietnam, the country might have been little the worse for wear. Unfortunately, not all "foreign" religions "visiting" Vietnam came from the East.

Chapter Six
Cross and Double-Cross

The influence of Christianity in general and Catholicism in particular began the minute Marco Polo set foot in Vietnam and would continue up to, and beyond, the founding of the Cao Dai religion in the first half of the 20th century.

So far as the Christian record of conquest is concerned, where the bloody Crusaders left off, equally ruthless colonizers took up the same banner, a banner blessed by the Pope time and again.

The Kingdom of Prester John

The Medieval Western lust for land and glory came from many sources, not the least of which was a myth that began circulating even before Marco Polo returned from his journey with fantastic tales of rich Eastern lands.

From the 12th century onward, about the time the Crusaders were just getting started, a tale began to be told and retold in Europe of a Christian Knight named Prester John who had crusaded into the Holy Land and had carved (literally *carved*, with sword and battle axe!) a vast kingdom for himself.

Prester John soon came to represent the fantasy of every Crusader — that of building themselves a kingdom in a foreign land.

Over the centuries, a few European adventurers would actually succeed in realizing this dream. Most wouldn't.

Down through the years, the legend of Prester John continued to grow, and change, depending on the agenda of whomever was doing the telling.

In his 14th century book, *Travels*, Marco Polo makes mention of *his* version of Prester John: a fabulously wealthy Christian ruling a vast empire somewhere in Africa and/or Asia. According to Marco Polo, Prester John was originally an Asian "Tartar" who had become Emperor of Abyssinia (Ethiopia).

Tales of this particular Prester John were still circulating when explorer Vasco da Gama (1469–1524) rounded the Cape of Good Hope, opening India and the Far East to European traders.

The fact that the actual whereabouts of Prester John's empire (like Atlantis) was always in dispute never dissuaded Crusaders or later European freebooters of every sort from seeking out his kingdom; they sought Prester John and personal profit from the Ugandan wilds of Africa, to lands in the Far East . . . such as *Vietnam*.

FYI: One of the more interesting speculations is that the legend of Prester John was a complete fabrication, a clever propaganda campaign.

Who would profit by such a bald-faced lie?

The first suspect in this conspiracy theory (as in *most* conspiracy theories!) is the Vatican, who did indeed freely use the myth of Prester John to stimulate the fantasy that any (and all!) good Christian Crusaders would be able to pluck themselves a personal kingdom from the Holy Land . . . so long as a steady stream of booty from these new kingdoms kept rolling in to Rome.

A second possible "conspirator" was Marco Polo himself — a businessman first, explorer second. His much-embellished tales of lavish wealth waiting in Asia helped him attract eager investors for his future ventures.

Other "conspirators" who might have benefited from spreading the legend of Prester John include those ever-elusive champions of free enterprise, the Illuminati.

And a new set of players whom we shall discuss in a minute, the Jesuits.

––––––

Whatever the origin of the Prestor John myth, whoever the *agent provocateurs* with a hidden agenda active in spreading such disinformation, the fact remains the myth of Prester John, stories of fabulous wealth and worldly glory to be found in "eastern lands," inspired generations of European explorers, entrepreneurs, and opportunistic empire builders.

The Jesuits

Inevitably, wherever Catholic "Conquistadors" (to borrow from the Spanish) waded ashore, sundry missionaries — the flotsam and jetsam of fanatical faith — inevitably washed ashore with them, eager to "civilize" (i.e., "soften up") native populations.

Monotheism's tried-and-true methodology: Conquer with sword, crush with bludgeon, control with the Book!

Where Buddhism and Taoism had intermingled *sans* incident, easily incorporating indigenous animist beliefs of the Vietnamese into their teachings, Christianity was content to crush.

The more dedicated (i.e., fanatical) those Christian missionaries, the more efficient that crushing.

And no Christians were more "efficient" than the Jesuits.

"Jesuits" is the name given members of *the Society of Jesus*, an order of Catholic monks founded in 1534 by Ignatius Loyola and given the blessing of Pope Paul III in 1540. Founded to combat the Protestant "revolt" (i.e., the Reformation), Jesuits wasted no time acquiring a reputation for ruthless efficiency:

"Through its discipline, organization, and methods of secrecy, [the Society of Jesus] acquired such power that it came into conflict with both the civil and religious authorities." (Brewer, 1959:587)

So notorious in their "efficiency" did the Jesuits become in so short a time that a *Jesuit* or *Jesuitical person* came to mean a "deceiver" or "prevaricator." (Ibid.)

FYI: Nazi SS Chief Himmler so admired the Jesuits that he reportedly modeled his "elite" SS Troopers after the Jesuits.

In short order, rulers throughout Europe were objecting to the Jesuits' heavy hand and to their literal "holier-than-thou" attitude.

When repeated demands to the Pope to bring the Jesuits under control fell on deaf ears, Jesuits were banned in France in 1762, and expelled from Portugal in 1759, and Spain in 1767.

Finally, the Jesuit Order was suppressed by Pope Clement XIV in 1773, only to be turned loose again on the world by Pius VII in 1814.

Jesuits roamed (or is that *"Romed"*?) the globe, indoctrinating "ignorant savages and heathen" with the word of God as interpreted by the Vatican. As a result, Jesuits were soon recognized — and *feared!* — from the Amazon to Asia.

Wherever European ships landed, there was a Jesuit walking down the gangplank.

In the Far East, Jesuits traded in their trademark black robes for saffron robes, a color Asian people would mistake for Buddhist robes.

This subtle subterfuge (one of many) helped Jesuits get a foot in the door of the homes of unsuspecting Buddhists, allowing them to spread their unique version of the gospel.

For Jesuits, any means was justified in the service of their ultimate goal: bringing heathen souls to God . . . while expanding the influence of their Society . . . not necessarily in that order.

––––––

FYI: Another one for you conspiracy buffs: The founding of the Cao Dai religion was a plot by Jesuits to fuse together the diverse religions of Vietnam into one religion, which would then — slowly and meticulously, as was the Jesuit way — be cleansed of heathen (i.e., Eastern) influences and brought into the Vatican fold.

The extreme version of this conspiracy theory is that the Jesuits had finally become so full of themselves that they decided to set up their own church . . . the Cao Dai! (More on this in "Cult and Occult.")

––––––

Though there were many qualities the Vietnamese admired about the orthodox Catholic Church, Catholicism has always remained the "foreign" religion of European "invaders."

Despite this, Catholicism would still prove a major influence on the founding of the Cao Dai, as well as on Vietnamese history in general, both before and after WWII.

In 1954 a great number of Catholics from North Vietnam fled to South Vietnam after the fall of Hanoi. This resulted in South Vietnam having the strongest Catholic population in Asia outside of the Philippines. This fact would have a major influence on tensions between Catholics and non-Catholics (Buddhists, and to a lesser extent Cao Dai) in the early 1960s, leading to open warfare in the streets, and culminating in the overthrow and assassination of South Vietnam's *Catholic* President.

But Catholic fanatics and factions — renegade or otherwise — were not the only Christians to impact Vietnam.

Cult and Occult

"Cult is what the big religion calls the little religion, what the old religion calls the new." (Lung and Prowant, 2001:110)

Today, the words "cult" and "occult" mean pretty much the same thing. However, during the Middle Ages, the words were opposites.

Back then "cult" referred to any religious belief or ritual approved of by The Vatican: "Cult" = "Church."

"Occult," on the other hand, meant "hidden" and "not revealed," hence not receiving the blessing of the Vatican. "O" = "not," i.e., "Not-Church."

Thus any type of religious activity not approved by the Catholic Church, (i.e., anything Protestant) was "occult," and had a target painted on its butt.

Over the course of years, many "occult" groups became recognized and respectable Protestant sects (Baptists, Lutherans, etc.) and, like Catholics, they too sent missionaries into Southeast Asia.

Let us assume that all these missionaries "meant well" and that their hearts were in the right place, even if their heads were up their . . . .

As we were saying, many non-Catholic Christian groups sent missionaries to Vietnam.

In addition to these Christian groups, as soon as Vietnam came under the control of the French, many religious "fringe" groups also sent missionaries to Vietnam.

These included Spiritualists, Theosophists, the likes of Aleister Crowley, and our old friends, the Illuminati — resurrected in France in the 17th century as the Guerinists, so-called for their "founder" Peter Guerin. (Brewer, 1959:494)

Chapter Seven
The Call to "The High Tower"

"Founded in the 1920s, Caodaism is a hybrid of Buddhism, Taoism, Confucianism, Vietnam spiritism, Christianity, Hinduism and Islam. The result is a jumbled code of ethics and tenets that has attracted more than three million followers despite the Vietnamese government's control of religion. In addition to calling on spirits, Cao Dai believers practice priestly celibacy, vegetarianism and the worship of ancestors. The religion emphasizes morality and frowns on material luxuries, lust and deceit." (Dao Thu Hien, 1997:47)

The Cao Dai religion officially came into being on November 18th, 1926 in a dramatic ceremony held in Tay Ninh, just northwest of Saigon. This elaborate ceremony, drawing more than 50,000 people, saw the seating of Le Van Trung as Cao Dai's first "Pope."

Within four short years of its founding, Cao Dai numbered more than 500,000 members by conservative estimate and would soon boast over 1,000,000 followers, fully 1/8th the population of what would eventually become South Vietnam.

Cao Dai was the right religion in the right place at the right time, a timely revelation perfect for an oppressed people looking for something new and empowering.

Under the French colonial authority, Catholicism had to a great extent come to overshadow both Vietnam's indigenous animism and the *Tam giao*. Yet Catholicism would always remain the religion of the oppressor.

Keeping what he admired in the French conquerors, the prophet of this new religion would borrow much — and shamelessly! — from Catholicism.

The Prophet

Ngo Van Chieu (1878-1932), aka Ngo Minh Chieu, was a minor Vietnamese official working for the French Indochina colonial administration.

Chieu had been well-educated under the colonial system and spoke both Vietnamese and French and possibly additional regional languages such as Chinese.

Widely read in both Eastern and Western philosophy and religion, Chieu had a decidedly mystical bent to him that led him to a fascination with spiritism.

Keep in mind that Vietnam already had a rich tradition of animist spirit worship, which Chieu was undoubtedly familiar with, as well as being conversant with Taoist spiritism imported from China.

Perhaps most important, Chieu's interest in spiritualism was encouraged by several of his *French* friends, themselves caught up in the Spiritualism Movement sweeping through America and Europe at the time, especially in Paris.

This Western Spiritualist Movement had initially been championed by such notables of the time as Sir Arthur Conan Doyle (1859–1930), creator of *Sherlock Holmes*, and by Doyle's magician friend Harry Houdini (b. 1874).

Houdini would later turn against the movement and pursue a dogged campaign exposing fake mediums and sundry spiritualists claiming the ability to communicate with the dead through séances.

Ironically, Houdini died the same year, 1926, that just such a séance in Vietnam gave birth to a new Spiritualism-based religion — The Cao Dai.

Hoan Vu Speaks!

Part of Chieu's weekly routine was to get together on a regular basis to conduct séances with a group of his Vietnamese friends, all intellectuals.

During one especially intense séance, a spiritual entity calling itself "Cao Dai" appeared and commanded Chieu to declare a new religion.

FYI: The word "Cao Dai" literally means "the High(est) Tower" and is a Chinese-Taoist euphemism for "Tao," the One. (See "*Lao Giao*: Taoism.")

Recall that in Taoism, "Tao," the one all-pervading and permeating force in the universe, is impersonal.

When most Vietnamese speak of this impersonal force they call it simply, *Hoan Vu*, "the Universe," without attributing any personality or preference to it.

For those with a less abstract view of the universe, those who perceive Tao as more "personal" and "deliberate" in its actions, Tao becomes *Con Tao*, "the Maker." Thus the Tao is perceived according to each person's understanding. To some the impartial "essence" of the universe, to others, Tao becomes "deified" into a personal god: *Dang Tao Hoa* or *Hoa Nhi*, both of which means "the Creator" and "God."

Many simply "split the difference" and refer to Tao, God, or *whatever* as *Huyen Co*, "the Great Mystery," or *Cau do*, "a riddle," "a conundrum."

For Chieu, an even greater riddle had just presented itself: "The Great Mystery" had just spoken!

The Plot?

While Chieu does not initially appear to have been overtly political, he was nonetheless a member of a mixed French-Vietnamese Freemason's lodge, and reportedly a card-carrying member of at least one Vietnamese *hoi kin*, secret society.

This association has, of course, led to speculation as to Chieu's real motivation, whether he had actually received a revelation from a "higher source," or at least believed it himself, or if on the other hand, Chieu, or one or more of his inner circle of friends, were actually receiving their "revelations" from a purely *Earthly* source.

In other words, who was behind this "plot" to form a new religion? Had Chieu literally sold his soul for the dubious privilege of kissing the sacred black stone of French Illuminism?

If true, Chieu's Cao Dai would not be the last 20th century "cult" to be inspired, bankrolled, and/or manipulated by shadowy puppet-masters: secretive societies with hidden agendas, or yet another "rogue" faction of the world intelligence community.

FYI: Since over 900 people of Jim Jones' *People's Temple* committed suicide in Guyana, South America in 1978, more than one connection has been discovered linking the killer cult to the CIA. (Vankin, 1992:149)

Likewise, the infamous Unification Church (aka "the Moonies") that gained worldwide attention (and millions of followers) throughout the 80s via what has been called "cult mind-control," was discovered to have been founded and funded by the South Korean version of the CIA.

Closer to home, but no less bizarre: In October, 1989, when Louis Farrakhan, head of the so-called *Nation of Islam*, announced at a press conference held in Washington, DC, that he had been "beamed" aboard a gigantic UFO "Mother Wheel" secretly orbiting the Earth, many speculated that Farrakhan had been the "victim" of a clever CIA (?) plot designed to further unhinge his mind. (Lung and Prowant, 2001:161)

And these are only the latest of cults and cult leaders conceivably inspired and controlled from behind "the Black Curtain."

———

Was Chieu the willing (or unwilling) front man for a shadowy group with a hidden agenda? But if so, which group?

Any good detective will tell you the only thing worse than having no suspects for a crime is having *too many!*

Did the Illuminati have a black-gloved hand in Chieu's revelation, to the point of even loaning Chieu their All-Seeing Eye? Or was it the Jesuits — with or without the blessing of the Vatican — intent on establishing a "Prester John" kingdom in the Far East? What about some sinister Eastern Cadre: Japanese Black Dragons, Chinese Triads, or one of the many Vietnamese secret societies, all with agendas political, profitable . . . or both? Perhaps, as it is rumored, Chieu actually met — and was inspired and initiated by — that international rogue, Aleister Crowley? We'll probably never know for certain.

———————

What we do know for certain is that, from its humble beginnings, Chieu's Cao Dai grew at a phenomenal rate to become an influential player in Vietnamese politics in general and in the lives of those who became Cao Dai in particular.

The Process

In keeping with the Vietnamese tradition of the *Tam Giao*, Chieu's new Cao Dai religion was "Universalist," declaring that all religions are really just varying aspects of the one true religion, The Cao Dai. Cao Dai's stated purpose was thus to unify all the religions of the world.

FYI: Other "universalists" had attempted this before, including the 19th century *Baha'i* of Persia, and the modern-day Unification Church.

In fact, the uniting of all religions under one banner is said to be at the top of the Illuminati's list of things to do today.

———————

Following Chieu's initial revelation, during subsequent séances the "Cao Dai" spirit continued to instruct Chieu on additional tenets and details of the new religion, from how to conduct worship, to what symbol should represent the new church: the old *Illuminati* standby, the All-Seeing Eye.

As already mentioned, the new Cao Dai religion borrowed freely, not just from Catholicism, but from the *Tam Giao* as well:

"The substantial Chinese cultural influence in Vietnam is evidenced in the fundamental similarity of Cao Dai to religious Taoist sectarianism in its spiritism, political overtones, and colorful liturgy." (Eliade 1987, Vol 2:72)

Service and Sacrifice

According to Cao Dai, we gain merit through service and through sacrifice. In Vietnamese this is *Vai*, literally "to bow with joined hands."

Cao Dai rituals are performed in *den chua*, temples and pagodas, four times each day and on festival days that are celebrated with great fanfare.

These rituals include prayers, chants, and symbolic sacrificial offerings of incense, tea, and wine, all presented with highly stylized ceremony.

Cao Daists also symbolically sacrifice the *Tam Sinh*, "The Three Beasts:" Bull, Goat, and Pig, corresponding respectively to doing away with negative attitudes, out-of-control appetites, and counterproductive actions.

We sacrifice the Bull when we give up the negative and stubborn attitudes that hold us back. "Bull-headed," get it?

Sacrificing the Goat means giving up those appetites (physical and mental) that hold us back. (Goats "eat" anything, right?)

Likewise, sacrificing the Pig means refraining from actions that are detrimental (i.e., we need to figuratively — and literally! — stop "wallowing in the mud" of this world).

Through self-discipline, the *Ngu quan*, "the Five Senses," are brought under control as we gain mastery over the *That tinh*, "the Seven Passions:" Lust, Anger, Fear, Hate, Love, Joy, and Sorrow.

The idea here is that *any* passion, taken to extremes, can be deadly. For example, excessive love *blinds* us as surely as excessive anger, excessive joy intoxicates as easily as does hate, while excessive fear and sorrow can both paralyze us.

That tinh discipline increases our *sinh lurk*, our "vital life force" that is seen as being identical to the Taoist *Chi*.

In turn, increasing our *Chi* (actually increasing our *perception* of the *Chi* that is everywhere, always, and perfect) helps cleanse our *Than tri* ("spirit and intelligence").

Persevering in *That tihn* discipline, we ultimately gain *Phep Mau*, a "mysterious power" identified directly with the Cao Dai spirit.

———

The goal of Cao Dai is to (re)establish a balance between *Coi Nay*, "This World" (i.e., the material world, *Vat Gio*), and *Lai Sinh*, "the Next World," the spirit realm, sometimes referred to as *Kiep sau*, "the Afterlife."

Having (re)established a link with the world(s) beyond this one, upon death, we take our honored place in a grand celestial hierarchy of which this Earthly life is but a pale imitation.

Other Cao Daists believe they will return to life, after a respite in "Heaven," reincarnated, their destiny (*Kiep so*) determined by their individual *Nghiep bao* — Karma.

An elaborate Catholic-inspired hierarchy headed by a Cao Dai Pope, Cardinals, and Archbishops, priests and nuns interprets and administers these beliefs.

In addition to this traditional clergy, gifted mediums are also important within the Cao Dai; hardly surprising considering it was a sèance that launched the Cao Dai movement in the first place.

Séances and Saints

Formal séances within the Cao Dai are held separately from other ceremonies and are restricted to specific occasions and to recognized mediums given the blessing of the Cao Dai hierarchy.

Despite rules discouraging séances not approved by the "Holy See," new revelations gained from "unofficial" séances inspired the creation of numerous "sub-sects" within the Cao Dai church. (Ibid., 73)

Some of these revelations came from natural spirits inhabiting "worlds" adjoined to our own, while other otherworldly communications came from Cao Dai "saints" who had "crossed over" to the other side.

In addition to the "Most High" Cao Dai, the Cao Dai religion recognizes a great company of saints.

In an effort to bridge the world of the living with the spirit world, séances are held during which spirits of the dead can be petitioned for aid and advice.

The Earthly lives and works of these enshrined saints can also be studied and meditated upon to help guide us along the path of life.

In addition to the revered founders of the *Tam giao*: Guatama Buddha, Lao-Tzu, and Confucius, other Asian notables such as Sun Yat-Sen, the first (and last!) President of China, and Vietnamese poet Nguyen Binh Khiem are recognized as saints.

But Cao Dai does not just recognize Eastern saints.

Western religious figures such as Jesus and Muhammad, as well as Western philosophers and scientists such as Pericles, political figures ranging from Julius Caesar to Joan of Arc, Lenin and Churchill, and even writers and entertainers such as French author Victor Hugo (author of *Les Miserables*, 1862) and silent film star Charlie Chaplin have been canonized by the Cao Dai.

All of these powerful personalities are held up by the Cao Dai as examples to be emulated, "Masters" to be honored, studied, and meditated upon, in order to help us lead better lives:

"They look to the spirits of such people because their strong personality traits are models to others." (Dao Thu Hien, 1997:47)

Power and Politics

The Cao Dai "Holy See" headquarters is Cao Dai's "sacred city" of *Tay Ninh* (southern Vietnam, on a tributary of the *Van Co Tay* River, 65 miles (105 km) northwest of Saigon, which was renamed *Ho Chi Minh* City in 1975. This region has a mixed population of Vietnamese, Cambodian Khmer, Chinese, and a Cham Islamic minority. It was here in the late 1920s that the newly-formed Cao Dai religion set up a large temple housing their Holy See and many administrative offices. The Cao Dai Holy See hierarchy's job was/is to oversee both the spiritual and secular welfare of its congregation.

Much to the alarm of the French colonial authorities, the Cao Dai soon came to dominate the entire area by amassing considerable agricultural and business holdings.

Inevitably, as the religion's wealth and influence increased, so did the envy — and hatred — of their foes and the fear of their French keepers.

FYI: Of course, Cao Dai would not be the first novel religious sect to run afoul of authorities who feared their rapid growth and growing influence. Recall that a similar scenario is what spelled doom for the *Yamabushi* monks in Japan. (See "From Buddha to Black Dragons.")

Similar envy (equal parts fear and greed) had brought down such controversial religious orders as the *Shao-Lin* of China and the *Knights Templars* in Europe.

During the decades of strife between 1930 and 1975, Cao Dai exercised effective control over most of the province around Tay Ninh.

Ironically, while Cao Dai's stated goal was "universalism," the "cult" was immediately looked upon with suspicion by the French colonial authorities who worried — and rightly so — the new movement might become a rallying point for nationalists, and/or might be infiltrated and taken over by more openly militant groups, such as the vocal Buddhist *Hoa Hao* after 1939, and the *Viet Minh* following their emergence in 1941.

In fact, from the day of its founding, *Canh cay* (literally "a branch of a tree"), breakaway sects and cliques began spinning off from the central Cao Dai organization.

On paper, each Cao Dai *Den chua* temple was ruled over by a *Tru Tri* abbot responsible for the actions of both the monks and the civilian *De tur* disciples under him.

But, in addition to such temples, "unauthorized" Cao Dai-inspired séance parties and political "discussion" groups began springing up, all identified in one way or another — if only in the paranoid minds of the French authorities — as "Cao Dai."

It soon became increasingly difficult for the central Cao Dai Holy See to keep track of the activities of each and every one of these "splinter groups" and "rogue factions," each busy chasing after their respective mystical or political agenda.

Inevitably some of these "Cao Dai" groups ran afoul of the French colonial authorities and it began to reflect back negatively on the main body of the Cao Dai church.

The Cao Dai fell under even more suspicion and scrutiny when Cao Dai *kung-fu* martial arts schools, already popular, began to flourish following the Cao Dai's formation of its own Self-Defense Force militia in 1943.

One of the problems was that various Cao Dai groups — especially martial arts *Quang Boi* — were constantly being misidentified as "militant" and "political."

This misperception was fed by the fact that other groups, political factions and rival religious groups, often found it convenient to masquerade as Cao Dai — sometimes in order to hide their true identities and agendas, and/or in order to further drag Cao Dai's name through the mud.

Some of the Cao Dai's critics thought the Cao Dai were doing *too much,* while others accused the Cao Dai of not doing *enough!*

Already entrenched religious groups in Vietnam felt threatened by the upstart Cao Dai's "universalist" teaching that was tempting away their most loyal parishioners, i.e., the parishioners with the deepest *purses.*

Political groups, on the other hand, accused Cao Dai of doing *too little.* Seems they didn't appreciate Cao Dai's *laissez-faire,* live-and-let-live attitude, when it came to politics.

Cao Dai exercised considerable influence over its members, many of whom were coveted Vietnamese intellectuals. Thus many political groups — both those fighting French rule and later those actively opposing the Diem government in the 1950s and 60s — felt that Cao Dai leaders should do more to support "the Resistance."

While basically supporting nationalism, for the most part Cao Dai played the peacemaker and tried to get along with everyone by making alliances with contending factions — some violently opposed to one another!

Despite a valiant effort, from the day of its founding, Cao Dai couldn't steer clear of politics.

———

"C" comes between "B" and "D" in the encyclopedia, so when you look up "Cao Dai" you'll find it stuck halfway between "Buddhists" and "Diem." And that's exactly what happened in the 1950s, when the Cao Dai found themselves caught up in the "war" between "militant" Buddhists and Ngo Dinh Diem, the new *Catholic* President of South Vietnam.

Buddhists from Hell!

After 1939, Cao Dai were often mistaken for a controversial Buddhist sect also concentrated in the Tay Ninh area.

The *Phat Giao Hoa Hao* (*Hoa Hao*, for short) was formed in 1939 by Buddhist reformer *Huynh Phu So*. Along with the Cao Dai, Hoa Hao was one of the first 20th century Vietnamese "Resistance groups" to openly stand up against the French, and then the Japanese . . . and then the French *again!*

FYI: Buddhism teaches non-violence. Despite this fact, Buddhist teachings — stressing a calm detachment towards life in general and death in particular — became the guiding philosophy for some of the fiercest *warriors* on the planet, including the *Shao-Lin* monks of China, the *Yamabushi* and later the *ninja* of Japan, and perhaps best known of all, medieval samurai:

"The code of the samurai was a mixture of Shintoism, Buddhism, and Confucianism. Shintoism taught the warriors that they were descendants of divine beings and that upon death they, too, would become 'gods.' From Buddhism they learned to accept the transitory, fragile nature of life and to view death as crossing into another plane of existence. From Confucianism came the concept of absolute loyalty to their lord." (Naito, 1989:20)

More on similarities between the beliefs — and blows! — shared by samurai and Cao Dai warriors in the next section.

––––––

While ostensibly non-violent "Buddhist," the Hoa Hao wasted little time running afoul of the French authorities.

Though originally formed to oppose the French, the Hoa Hao came into existence just in time to "welcome" the invading Japanese army in 1941.

Around this same time, a relatively unknown troublemaker by the name of *Ho Chi Minh* formed another guerilla "Resistance group," the *Viet Minh*, for the express purpose of expelling the Japanese invaders.

In 1943, after much debate, the Cao Dai established its own "Self-Defense Force," designed to protect its members.

The Cao Dai would maintain this "militia" up through the mid-1950s. With this formidable force protecting them, Cao Dai effectively created what has been described as "a monastery-fortress in south-central Vietnam." (Eliade 1987, Vol. 26:1029)

The Cao Dai's militia had been formed for "self defense." However, the old adage holding true that: "The best defense is a good offense," in short order units identifying themselves as Cao Dai were found fighting alongside Hoa Hao and Viet Minh against the Japanese.

In addition to their army "regulars," Cao Dai had spawned a score of martial arts "clubs," some of which were thinly disguised guerilla training centers.

FYI: Politically oriented guerilla/subversive movements "hiding behind religion" are nothing new, whether in the East or in the West.

In 13th century Japan, the *Yamabushi* monks in Japan were burned out, as were the *Shao-Lin* monasteries in 17th century China, both martial orders accused of training subversives.

To give the benefit of the doubt to both the Brothers of Shao-Lin and to the Yamabushi, and to the Cao Dai for that matter, any would-be "guerilla" worth his salt gets his training catch-as-catch-can. If this involves his "converting" (temporarily) to a religion, or even joining his enemy's army, so be it!

Nobody trains your sons as well as your enemy.

———

Viet Minh guerillas, Hoa Hao activists, and the Cao Dai militia continued to harass the Japanese until they finally laid down their samurai swords and pulled out in 1945.

No sooner did the Japanese depart than the French were back, eager to reassert control over their Indochinese "colonies."

———

With the end of World War II, the Cao Dai became a rallying point, a source of stability the people could trust. Thus, Cao Dai emerged from World War II a powerful "player" in Vietnamese politics.

Hoping to negotiate independence from the French, the Cao Dai and the Hoa Hao opted for "peace talks" with the French.

Further north, Ho Chi Minh had other ideas and, in 1946, his Viet Minh openly attacked the French. For the next eight years, the Viet Minh fought a guerilla campaign, mostly in northern Vietnam, against the increasingly weary French. Finally, in 1954, Viet Minh forces defeated French forces after a 55-day siege at *Dien Bien Phu*.

The following year, the French pulled out of Vietnam and Ho Chi Min's Viet Minh seized Hanoi, effectively taking control of "North Vietnam."

Nationwide elections were ordered by the United Nations but, rightly fearing that Communists would carry the day if honest elections were held in the south, Premier *Ngo Dinh Diem* (b. 1901) refused to hold elections and — with the backing of the United States — declared the independent Republic of South Vietnam.

FYI: This was the *unofficial* start of America's "Vietnam War."

———

We really do create our own problems.

In response to Diem's 1956 "coup" in South Vietnam, and with the blessing of Ho Chi Minh, the Communist-backed *Viet Nam Cong San* ("Viet Cong") guerilla army was formed in the south to oppose Diem and reunite North and South Vietnam.

———

Educated and indoctrinated under the French colonial authorities, Diem was a staunch Catholic and so wasted no time turning all non-Catholic Vietnamese into second-class citizens, alienating all other religious groups in Vietnam in record time.

During this time Diem was trying to present a unified front — literally and figuratively — to the world. No big surprise then that the Cao Dai's "middle-of-the-road" policy did nothing to endear them to Diem.

Diem was worried — and rightly so — that Communist *agents provocateurs* would infiltrate such groups, inciting them to support a coup, further weakening South Vietnam.

Thus, one of Diem's first official acts was to order these militias to disband. Rather than risk civil war in the south, the Cao Dai Holy See complied.

Again we can see the parallel between the Diem government's treatment of the Cao Dai and the way other regimes had dealt with similar groups such as the Shugendo-Yamabushi of Japan and the Shao-Lin of China.

Still not satisfied, Diem also forced Cao Dai's Pope *Pham Cong Tac* into exile.

Despite this crackdown, Cao Dai would have the last laugh and outlive Diem.

In 1961 Diem signed a treaty with the United States and massive economic and military aid started flooding into South Vietnam. On the surface, with the help of his U.S. handlers, Diem appeared every bit the strong and confident bulwark against the godless Communists to the north. Yet no amount of CIA media-spin could disguise the fact that Diem's own people had turned against him.

FYI: This is one of those examples where the nightly media reported on "the Big War," the big battles and bombing, while either myopically missing or else deliberately ignoring what was going on behind the Black Curtain.

To make matters worse, Diem began relocating Viets into the Central Highlands, displacing the 'Yards. The policy would ultimately lead to a bloody coup in 1964 in the Central Highlands led by the 'Yards resistance movement FULRO.

But, by 1964, Diem would be beyond caring.

Never underestimate the power of religion. Diem did and ultimately paid the price. Diem rubbed a lot of people wrong during his rule. But his worst mistake was pissing off the Buddhists.

Recall that in 1956 he'd ordered all private militias to lay down their arms. Whereas the Cao Dai had complied, at least on paper, the Hoa Hao openly defied Diem's order.

The Hoa Hao joined other Buddhists protesting Diem's harsh treatment of Buddhists — ironically the majority religion in Vietnam! When these protests fell on deaf ears, the Hoa Hao openly battled against Diem's regime. At least one American Buddhist followed Thich Quang Duc's example. (Loewen, 1995:236)

Diem was still in denial but the world began to suspect something was wrong in South Vietnam when in 1963 a Buddhist monk *Thich Quang Duc* calmly doused himself with gasoline and burned to death while stoically meditating in the streets of Saigon. Other Buddhist protesters followed his example of non-violent protest and likewise immolated themselves. Still other Buddhists were beaten, shot, and imprisoned for non-violent protests against Diem's regime.

But not everybody was ready to be Gandhi.

Some months after Thich Quang Duc's death, and just a few weeks before Diem's biggest backer John F. Kennedy was assassinated, Diem himself was killed in a coup led by *Buddhist* generals within his own army.

Chaos reigned in South Vietnam until Nguyen Van Thieu, one of the officers who helped overthrow Diem, finally took power in 1967. With the blessing and backing of the U.S., of course.

Thieu remained in power until 1975.

———

At the time of Diem's death in 1963, the Hoa Hao controlled several southern and western provinces in South Vietnam. In January 1964, the Hoa Hao helped form the Buddhist umbrella organization *the United Buddhist Church*.

This is the beginning of what is called "the Buddhist Struggle Movement."

The Buddhist Struggle Movement would inadvertently contribute to the proliferation of Vietnamese marital arts since martial arts gatherings and clubs were perfect places for would-be guerillas to gather, not only to use as a cover, but also in order to acquire needed martial skills. To illustrate how extensive was this practice: in April 1964, ARVN intelligence reported that over 3,000 Buddhist "militants" were training in martial arts at the *Quang Trung* Judo School in Saigon.

The influence of the Buddhist Struggle Movement began to wane in the late 1960s as many of its members and supporters, including some Hoa Hao units joined the umbrella guerilla organization, the National Liberation Front.

Still the Hoa Hao would remain a powerful independent force in Vietnam politics until the Communists came to power in 1975.

The Cao Dai Since 1975

Cao Dai was immediately banned when Communists took over in 1975. A high proportion of Cao Dai churches were confiscated and its clergy ordered to hang up their robes. Those refusing to comply were arrested.

For a time, Cao Dai ceased to exist . . . at least openly.

In reality, Cao Dai continued to be practiced secretly, surviving underground with privately held séances, hidden rituals, and prayer meetings.

As we will see in the next section, Cao Dai martial arts also not only survived this dark period, but actually grew stronger, both in Vietnam and abroad as Vietnamese fled Communist rule.

The mass exodus from South Vietnam as Saigon fell scattered Vietnamese around the globe. As these Vietnamese fled their homeland, they took Cao Dai and Cao Dai kung-fu with them.

By 1985 over 20 Cao Dai worship centers had sprung up in Vietnamese refugee communities around the world.

By the 1990s Cao Dai worldwide numbered more than two million, with the majority of those adherents in Vietnam, Cambodia, France and the United States.

———

Cao Dai in Vietnam weathered the Communist monsoon.

Finally, in June 1997, the Vietnamese government gave the Cao Dai religion official sanction, legitimizing it in the eyes of the Communist leaders.

———

Today, in Tay Ninh, about 40 percent of the province's 916,000 people are Cao Dai believers, and the number is expanding every year, according to a spokesman for the Vietnamese government's Religious Affairs Committee in Tay Ninh. (Dao Thu Hien, 1997:47)

Today, Cao Dai is practiced in about half of Vietnam's provinces.

Worldwide, not only has Cao Dai prospered, but it has also given birth to a number of Cao Dai spin-off "cults," both East and West.

One even finds "secret" Cao Dai members: Buddhists, Taoists, and even self-identified Christians, using Cao Dai meditation techniques to speed their own quest to pierce the great mystery of the High Tower.

Not surprisingly, many South Vietnamese saw the fall of Saigon as the end of the world.

History has decided otherwise.

In fact, so far as Vietnamese martial arts are concerned, nothing could have been better since this mass exodus from South Vietnam helped "scatter" Vietnamese culture in general and *Cao Dai kung-fu* in particular far and wide!

Section III
Can Qua: "Shield and Spear"

"Tricks well-mastered are called techniques. Techniques half-learned are merely tricks." (Ralf Dean Omar, *Death on Your Doorstep: 101 Weapons in the Home*, 1993:21)

According to tradition, the 29th Buddhist Patriarch *Bodhidharma* (called *Tamo* by the Chinese, and *Daruma* in Japan) established the *Shao-lin* Order in Hunan Province, China around 588 CE.

A true taskmaster, Bodhidharma set the *Lo-han*, monks of Shao-lin, to a strict regimen of exercises soon dubbed "the 18 Hands of Lo-han." These 18 simple movements became the "original" kung-fu art of *Lo-han Chuan*, (literally "Monk's fist").

While originally kept "secret" from the outside world, inevitably Shao-lin martial arts began filtering out of the monastery and into the hands of soldiers, secret societies, and subversive movements.

Before long, the Shao-lin Order ran afoul of the new Manuch Emperor in 1644 and the monastery at Hunan was destroyed and the Brothers scattered. And their martial arts scattered with them.

Today all martial arts schools in China, and in fact, most martial arts schools throughout the Far East, take pride — and pains! — to trace themselves back to Bodhidharma and the Lo-han of Shao-lin.

From Shao-lin, Chinese "kung-fu" (more correctly called "*Wushu*," literally war art) spread far and wide, taken up and taught by the Chinese military and by a score of Chinese secret societies and subversive political and religious "cults" down through the centuries.

For example, the bloody "Boxer Rebellion" of 1900, China's first large-scale popular uprising directed against foreign imperialists — *including the French* — was led by cultists who taught their followers kung-fu Wu-Shu.

The Boxer Rebellion was spearheaded by a secret society/cult known as *Yi Ho Ch'uan* ("Fists of Righteous Harmony") aka "the Boxers" because of their use of what Europeans saw as "shadow-boxing," i.e., kung-fu Wu-Shu "forms" training.

Like the Cao Dai who came after them, the Boxers preached a blend of politics and religion, freely mixing Confucian, Buddhist, and Taoist ideas.

Though "the Boxer Rebellion" was eventually crushed and its leader executed, the Boxers helped inspire a half dozen similar "cults" inside China and abroad. These included political and religious groups, as well as secret societies and out-and-out criminal conspiracies such as the infamous "Red Spears."

The Chinese "Red Spears" of the 1920s had nothing to do with being "red" Communists; rather "red" was a clear warning of their proclivity to spill blood with little provocation.

Red Spears combined politics with mystical mutterings and martial arts. But dabbling in subversive politics was only one of the Red Spears' many activities, activities they financed through a widespread and lucrative extortion racket. In this respect, the Red Spears more closely resembled the Sicilian Mafia than any modern politically motivated terrorist movement. (Laqueur, 1977:9)

FYI: Having previously fought groups like the Boxers and the Red Spears in China, it was no wonder the French colonial authorities in Vietnam reacted with alarm to the creation of the Cao Dai, a secretive "cult" that, at least on the surface, seemed to the French identical to dangerous Chinese subversives known to conveniently cloak their criminal agenda behind the Black Curtain of cultic religion.

Like all countries East or West, Vietnam had its indigenous forms of fighting — armed and unarmed.

In addition, down through the centuries an endless stream of welcome and unwelcome "visitors" to Vietnam — from the Chinese to the Japanese, Indian, Thai and European — all brought with them various styles of fighting . . . and down through the centuries the Vietnamese *fought* each and every one of these "visitors" at one time or another.

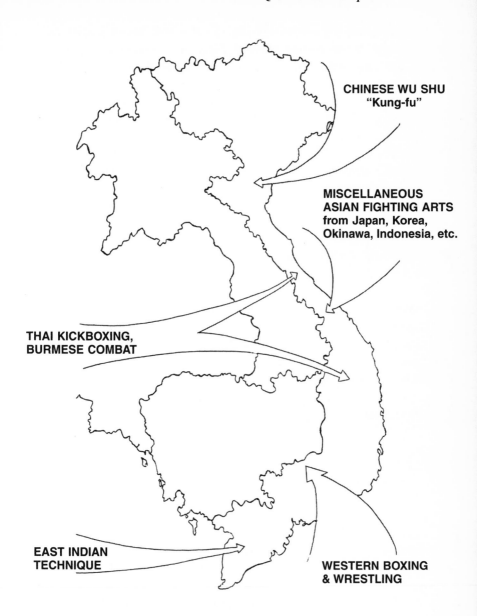

CHINESE WU SHU
"Kung-fu"

**MISCELLANEOUS
ASIAN FIGHTING ARTS**
from Japan, Korea,
Okinawa, Indonesia, etc.

**THAI KICKBOXING,
BURMESE COMBAT**

**EAST INDIAN
TECHNIQUE**

**WESTERN BOXING
& WRESTLING**

Figure 5
Martial Arts influences into/out of Vietnam

In war, you use whatever works, no matter if that tool, tactic, or technique was crafted by friend or foe.

The finest weapon is the one you pry from your dead enemy's hand.

That's exactly what the Vietnamese have always done.

Though suffering for centuries, overrun and oppressed by one invader after another, while its people and culture suffered overall, Vietnam's martial arts benefited.

FYI: This same scenario played out in Okinawa, the birthplace of what we now call *karate*.

When 17th-century Japanese conquerors made it punishable by death for an Okinawan to possess a weapon, Okinawan rebels began crafting weapons from everyday objects, giving the world *nunchakus* ("numb-chucks"), *tonfa* ("PR-24"), *sai*, and the *kama* sickle, as well as fierce fighting arts involving simple sticks and *bo*-staffs.

Okinawan fighters also ranged far and wide, learning *unarmed*, empty hand (Japanese *"kara"* = empty, *"te"* = hand) fighting techniques from Thai kickboxers, Korean *Hwarangdo* warriors, and Chinese *Wu-shu* artists, all of which they then blended with their indigenous *to-te* martial arts to create today's well-known karate styles: *shotokan, goju-ryu, isshin-ryu*, etc.

————

Vietnamese call martial arts *Vo Nghe*, "the Art of Fighting." This includes both armed and unarmed fighting. Often Vietnamese martial arts are referred to as *Vo Thuat*, "War Art," which is also used as slang to mean "boxing." Unarmed combat specifically is *Giap la ca*, or simply *La ca*, "Hand-to-hand."

Another term *chien* ("to fight") is attached to specific styles of fighting and/or to specific martial arts instructors, e.g., *Ho Chien*, Tiger (*Ho*) style of fighting (*chien*), or *Ho Chi Minh Chien*, literally the fighting style taught by "Master" Ho Chi Minh.

————

Learning any martial art is done in two phases: first, *appreciation* — understanding the roots and underlying meaning of the art —

and, second, *application* — putting what we've learned into actual practice.

As with the study of any martial art, in order to fully grasp Vietnamese *Vo Nghe* (henceforth simply called "kung-fu" for convenience's sake) we must begin our study by first acquiring the "mind-set," the *attitude*, of those Cao Dai warriors who have previously practiced, perfected and ultimately survived actual combat to pass their art along to us.

Having accomplished this initial *mental* step, we will then turn our undivided *attention* to mastering the physical *tools*, *techniques*, and *targets* specific to this life-saving (and life-taking) art.

Thus, through correct *attitude* and *attention* to detail we will learn, first, *appreciation* of Cao Dai kung-fu and then, second, the proper *application* of this art.

Having accomplished these two initial goals — the first mental, the second physical — only then can we proceed to *apply* what we have learned into a practical fighting "flow" by mastery of the *Mong Cop Mua Vo*. Tiger-style training form.

Chapter Eight
Cong Kem: The Two-Pronged Attack

"An open, relaxed hand can caress, grasp, and, when needed, close into a striking fist. Tightly clenched, a hand can only be used to strike. A tense mind is like a clenched fist: mental fears and tension prevent us from being fully functional." (Lung, 1998:43)

When a Cao Dai warrior attacks a foe, they attack not just that foe's body, but his *mind* as well. In fact, by directing the first prong of our attack into our foe's mind, we may eliminate the need to "follow through" with an actual physical attack. In this way, we accomplish what *Sun Tzu* proclaimed to be the consummate warrior skill: "To defeat an enemy without fighting is the greatest of skills."

Likewise, the Buddha once observed that our greatest weapon is in our enemy's mind, meaning an enemy's blinding anger, greed, hatred, and other negative emotions can all be turned to our advantage, allowing us to "get inside his head" in order to "throw him off his game." (See *"Am Hiem"* for more on this kind of "Psychological Warfare.")

Thus, Cao Dai kung-fu always employs a two-pronged attack: attacking both his body and his mind, knowing that the undermining of the one will surely bring down the other.

Fighting your enemy on both the *mental* battlefield as well as the *physical* battlefield requires mastery of "the Three Knows."

The Three "Knows"

"Some are born with a natural instinct for survival. Others spend their whole lives sweating to acquire the skills necessary to survive. An infuriating few just seem to muddle through! What we lack in instinct, we must make up for in study. Knowing yourself, knowing your foes and knowing your options in any given situation are the main prerequisites for survival in any threatening situation." (Omar, 2001:9)

According to Sun Tzu, if you know your enemy and you know yourself, in a hundred battles, you will never be defeated.

Sun Tzu goes on to say that if you know yourself, but are ignorant of your enemy, your chances of winning drop to fifty-fifty.

Finally, if you are as ignorant of your own abilities and resources as you are those of your enemy . . . you're *dead meat!*

Cao Dai call this art of "reading" people, *including yourself, Nhan lurc*, literally meaning "the strength of a person."

Know Yourself

"Nature has equipped us with all the senses and instincts we need to survive. Unfortunately, nature (society) has done its best to dull these senses and breed these instincts out of us." (Lung, 1998:45)

How does your enemy train and what does he train for?

When it comes to martial arts training, there is a big difference between training to lose weight and training to survive a tooth-and-nail encounter in the middle of the Southeast Asian jungle.

However, there shouldn't be a difference in the *intensity* of your training, no matter your ultimate "goal."

Cao Dai warriors practice *Chuot* (literally "to sharpen to a point"), constantly honing their existing physical and mental kung-fu skills while ever on the lookout for novel techniques.

For every second spent cutting with your sword, an hour must be spent beforehand honing that blade. It matters not if the blade be a blade of steel, or the metal of your mind!

———

Never show Kenny Rogers your hole card. Never telegraph your intent to an enemy. In other words, realistic martial artists never adopt "fancy" fighting stances that might telegraph their style of fighting to the enemy.

No mystery: An opponent standing tall, clenched fists at chest level, is probably a *boxer*. An attacker coming in low, his hands open, is probably a *wrestler*. Likewise, an *inexperienced kicker* will dance around lightly on his toes, or even raise his knee — all telegraphing his intent to kick.

Dedicated martial artists take the time to familiarize themselves with the positions and posturings of as many schools and styles of fighting as possible, in order to recognize the inherent strengths and weaknesses *all* martial arts possess.

Study to survive beforehand. As the ancient Chinese adage warns: "When the thunderclap comes, there is no time to cover your ears."

Know Your Enemy

"Knowing your own mind is only half the battle. The other half is discerning the mind-set of your enemy; his motivation and his weakness." (Skinner, 1995:27)

It's a waste of time to point a pistol at a fanatical suicide bomber, his body wrapped in explosives, and order him to "Halt, or I'll shoot!"

While it is not always possible to "know your enemy's heart" — whether the motivations of a street mugger, or the motivations of a fanatical suicide bomber — the more we can discern and learn about an enemy before we find ourselves locked into a life and death struggle with him, the better our odds of overcoming that enemy.

Look at your opponent. *Really* look at him.

Does your opponent's face give him away? Angry red or pale white? Is he sweating in fear and trying to swallow that lump of doubt in his throat? What is his motivation? What emotion rules him? Is he in it for money, or is his attack more personal?

Is he a simple "soldier," perhaps in a war he didn't choose? Or does he see himself as a "warrior"? The difference? A soldier's *job* is to *kill*. A warrior's *duty* is to *die*. A soldier can always take off his uniform and get a new *job*. A warrior has but one *duty*.

How much — and what kind of — training does your enemy have? Does he have years of *training* or years of *experience*?

While we're on the subject: Which do *you* have? Training or experience? There is a big difference between ten years training in a *dojo* (Japanese "training hall") and two years *fighting* tooth-and-nail in the jungles of Southeast Asia!

———

"No matter how formidable a foe might first appear, his body possesses the same basic vulnerabilities as does your body. No matter how frightening he might at first appear, his *intent* can be deciphered beforehand, his *techniques* of terror derailed, and, if need be, his ability to ever again do harm to you or anyone else can be destroyed." (Ibid. 53)

Know Your Environment

Everything works but not everything works all the time, every-where. Thus the Cao Dai warrior, like all dedicated martial artists, *trains to improvise* and constantly *updates his skills* in order to be able to adapt to combat in any type of time or clime.

As Ralf Dean Omar warns in his *Death on Your Doorstep* (1993:20), ". . . the perfect defense of yesterday might get you killed today."

While we study beforehand for the battlefield, battlefield deci-sions must be made on the spot. Master strategist Karl von Clauswitz (1780-1831) warned that, "No battle plan survives first contact with the enemy." In the same vein, Sun Tzu warned that there's nothing more dangerous than an Emperor trying to run a battle from a thousand miles way.

Remember: There is a big difference between sparring in the dojo, or even fighting in a boxing ring, versus finding yourself trapped in a kill-or-be-killed *Da chien* (battlefield combat) confrontation.

We learn our martial arts tactics and techniques in the dojo, but we test those tactics and techniques on the unforgiving battlefield of real life — no matter if that battlefield be the alleys of Atlanta or the hills of Afghanistan!

––––––

Having mastered ourselves with a firm hand, the mastery of any foe, any situation, then falls easily within our grasp.

Long Nhan: The Way of the Cao Dai Warrior

Within the overall Cao Dai organization existed a little known *hoi kin*, "secret society," whose mandate and mission was to train and maintain a ready cadre of Cao Dai *binh nhi* ("militia men," "private soldiers"). Like any secret society worth its salt, this *hoi kin* had its own requirements and rituals above and beyond those of its parent organization. To those within this fighting fraternity, it was the *Quang Boi* (kwang boi), "the Circle of Light."

Quang Boi: The Circle of Light

The literal translation of *Quang Boi* is the glowing circle of light said to surround the Buddha's head, what people in the West refer to as a "halo."

Others simply referred to this band of brothers as *Chiec nhan*, "The Ring," a term which includes not only their fellowship, but also the actual physical circle (ring/arena) where their martial skills might be tested.

"The Ring," in turn, was composed of many different *be lu*, "training cliques," bands that identified themselves with a particular village or region, a particular style of martial art, and/or who had dedicated themselves to the service of a particular *Bac pho*, "Master Instructor."

Like any good guerilla army, these various *be lu* operated as independent cells when it came to training, coming together whenever necessary to form larger units known as *xich sat* (literally "a chain"), designed to accomplish a particular end or enterprise.

All such *be lu* bands were, of course, ready at a moment's notice to respond to the call and rally to the defense of their central Cao Dai patron.

Trang Si: Braves of the Cao Dai

The word *Bach pho* literally means "white-haired," referring to a respected teacher and when applied to martial arts is synonymous with the Japanese *Sensei* and the Chinese *Sifu*.

The word *Bach pho* was also sometimes used to refer to *Quang boi* martial arts instructors since the word has a double meaning. On the one hand it means "white tiger," a reference to their power and ferocity. But, on the other hand, *Bach pho* can also mean "evil genius," "diabolical" and "ruthless," an obvious warning to any potential enemy.

When speaking directly to such a Master, the respectful *Cao sang*, "Noble man," or *Cao si*, "Learned man," are correct. The most used form of address for these Masters is *Chop bu*, which simply means "Head man." The *Chop bu* of a particular style of fighting is also referred to as *Chu*, "Master of the House."

Collectively, within the *Quang boi* such teachers are *Tien boi*, "The Elders."

Under these *Tien boi chu* are the rank and file known collectively as *Anh Ruot*, "Blood Brothers."

The term *Anh ruot* carries with it the implicit knowledge that these individuals are "made men," that they have already survived arduous testing and training (*toi thep*, literally "to harden steel") and have been granted *xuat dinh*, initiation (literally "to leave one's home") into the brotherhood.

These brothers are further subdivided into ranks of *bao huyuh* and *bao de*, "Elder brothers" and "Younger brothers," respectively.

Having been granted entrance into this elite brotherhood, each Cao
Dai warrior dedicates himself to serving (*cui chao*, literally "to bow
to someone") a particular *Cung* ("temple," "palace," or "house").

In many ways this is analogous to a Japanese samurai swearing
loyalty to a particular *Kan* (Japanese "House"), meaning a particular family, clan or dynasty.

Braves and Black Flags

Cao Dai Quang Boi warriors were known by many names, depending on who was doing the talking — friend or foe, whether being
lauded or cursed.

Not surprisingly, enemies of the Cao Dai felt threatened by the
Cao Dai's ready militia and often referred to Cao Dai warriors as *Ba
que*, "rogues and rascals," and as *du dao*, "highwaymen."

Quang Boi warriors were also referred to by others, and often by
themselves, as *Co den*, "Black flags." *Co den* banners had been
flown by Vietnamese pirates for centuries. Black flags were also traditionally raised over Vietnamese prisons to show a man — often a
pirate — had been put to death. Rather than refuting this association,
Cao Dai Quang Boi *encouraged* this association in their enemies'
minds by wearing black masks (i.e., "black flags") over their faces,
not unlike their Japanese Ninja and Chinese *Lin Kuei* cousins.

Speaking of the dreaded Chinese *Lin Kuei* "Forest Demons" from
whom the equally feared *Moshuh Nanren* assassins trace themselves,
Cao Dai Quang Boi warriors were often whispered themselves to
be *Yeu Quai* ("Ghost Demons") somehow conjured up by mysterious
Cao Dai *Bi thuat* magic.

To their friends and fellows, these Cao Dai warriors were simply
Trang si, "Braves," and *Dung si*, "Valiant men."

The Nine Virtues of Valiant Men

Like most elite warriors cadres, Cao Dai *Dung Si* held themselves
to a strict code of conduct, nine "virtues" know as *Hung hoai* (literally "something kept in one's heart").

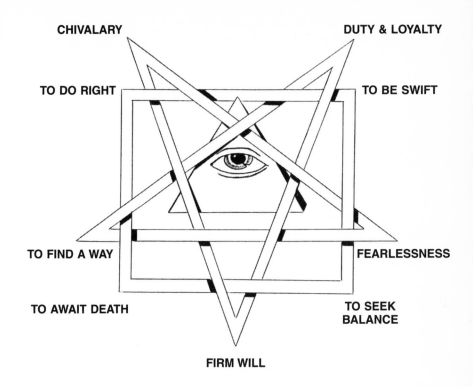

Figure 6
The Nine Virtues

(1) **Chivalry** (*hung hao*) is the first principle as well as the collective concept that bonded together the eight "virtues" that followed.

Like similar codes of conduct found amongst Western warrior orders such as the Knights Templars, and the code of *bushido* followed by Japanese samurai, the oath of chivalry taken by Cao Dai *Dung Si* held them to an ideal of social and moral correctness wherein their every action was meant to benefit those under their protection.

(2) **Duty and Loyalty** (*buoc long and long son*) included the fulfilling of social duties (*co nghi*), such as obligations to parents and

pasture, family and friends, and extended to a *Dung Si*'s obligation to his Cao Dai religion, his unbreakable loyalty to the brotherhood of the *Quang Boi* in general, and to his *be lu* Master in particular.

(3) **Fearlessness** (*dan di*) includes the characteristic of dam khi ("courageousness" and "daring"). This is often spoken of as possessing *chuy cot* (literally a backbone, and "to stand erect"), standing your ground in the face of danger.

(4) **Firm Will** (*nhue y*) is reflected in the *Dung Si*'s dedication and determination, his inner resolve reflected in his every action.

(5) **To Find a Way** (*tim c'ach*) means "to manage," to persevere until you find a way no matter the situation, no matter the danger; to do what must be done, to accomplish one's mission by any means necessary; to strive and to struggle (*phan dau*), often against impossible odds.

This is similar to the Japanese warrior concept of *Masakatsu*, which literally means "Victory by all means," by any means necessary.

————

An extreme example of *tim c'ach* occurred in 1988 when a leaky, 45-foot Vietnamese boat filled with 110 refugees set out for Malaysia from the Vietnamese port of Truc Giang.

Three days out, the boat broke down. After five days, the food and water ran out.

Spotting a Japanese freighter, some of the refugees tried swimming for the freighter but drowned.

Two weeks out, the boat was spotted by an American warship headed for the Persian Gulf. The Americans left six cases of canned meat, six gallons of fresh water and a map, before steaming away.

After the American ship abandoned them, one of the refugees, a former Vietnamese "Red Beret" paratrooper named *Phung Quang Minh* decided drastic measures were called for. Phung and the men who joined him on this desperate voyage, took charge.

This voyage was Phung's tenth attempt to escape Communist Vietnam. He'd already spent four years in prison for two similar escape attempts. He was a hard man about to make hard choices.

Having encountered the Americans, most on the boat expected

rescue within a few days. Phung nonetheless began rationing what little food there was. Days passed and no rescue came.

Twenty-eight days into the voyage, with no food or water left, Phung decided they would use the bodies of those already dead for food. Another week passed and, once this gruesome food source was exhausted, Phung instituted a lottery. The losers were quickly killed and slowly eaten.

FYI: Vietnamese pirates (*Thao tac*) refer to human flesh as "long pig."

After 37 days at sea, the refugee boat finally made landfall near Luzon in the Philippines.

Only 52 out of the original 110 refugees had survived.

But had it not been for the *tim c'ach* "ruthlessness" of Phung, none would have survived.

––––––––

Tim c'ach often calls for Cao Dai warriors to make tough choices. Knowing this, the virtue of *tim c'ach* is always to be tempered by the next virtue:

(6) **To Do Right** (*lam phai*). Each *Dung Si* must decide for himself what is the correct course of action, how to "do right." He of course has his brother warriors, as well as his spiritual and martial arts leaders to help guide him. But, ultimately, only he can make the decisions that will keep his thoughts and actions in accord with the ideal of *lam phai*.

FYI: Much of Cao Dai philosophy was influenced by Buddhism where, likewise, each person must decide for themself what is right and wrong.

For Cao Dai warriors, as for Buddhists in general, each decision in life must be tempered by concept of *phap che*, "The Law," meaning not only the prevailing law of any particular place and time, but also the Universal Law (in Sanskrit, *Dharma*) taught by the Buddha.

Buddha left behind his "Eight-Fold Path" of conduct consisting of: Right Views, Right Desires, Right Speech, Right Conduct, Right Livelihood, Right Endeavors, Right Mindfulness, and Right Meditation.

However, unlike Western monotheistic religions (one of which even has "religious police" looking over an adherent's shoulder to make sure they toe the party line), in Buddhism, as in Cao Dai, each individual must decide for themself what is right and what is wrong.

(7) **To Be Swift** (*lanh tay*). The term *lanh tay* literally means "to be swift-handed," that is, once having made a decision in accordance with *lam phai* and *phap che*, a Cao Dai warrior acts swiftly and decisively.

Implicit within the virtue of *lanh tay* is the prerequisite of *lanh tri*, being "quick-witted," and *mau chan*, to be "agile" and flexible of strategy.

(8) **To Seek Balance** (*phuc thu*). To seek "balance" is to actively campaign for justice (*cong dao*). The major component to this is to have *curong chi*, a word that means "strong will . . . and stronger memory!"

Phuc Thu sometimes required a warrior to avenge a wrong done to him or his. Thus, the Vietnamese have a saying: "*Mau phai tra mau!*," "Blood must be paid by blood!"

However, to prevent their warriors from taking indiscriminate vengeance, a *Quang-Boi* Master cautions his student, "You are not *Van hoi* (i.e., Fate, Destiny, Karma) . . . but you may be called upon to be her sword!"

(9) **To Await Death** (*cho chet*). The Cao Dai warrior had a duty to survive (*di ton*), to live to fight another day. However, when odds proved impossible, rather than risk capture (and under torture reveal information that might harm their brothers), Cao Dai warriors chose *phuc kiem* (literally "to fall upon one's sword").

Dung Si warriors often referred to this extreme as *dan quyet* (zan kwiet), meaning "to bite one's tongue off;" this includes both the physical act of killing oneself to avoid capture, as well as the deeper understanding that "Silence is golden," similar to the Mafia's *Omerta* code of silence, a determination to die before revealing any *Quang Boi* secrets.

———

For Cao Dai warriors, to trespass any one of these nine "virtues" was damnation, not only in this world (*coi nay*) but in the afterlife

(*Lai sinh*). In fact, the Cao Dai term *Chin Suo*, "the Nine Springs" was a euphemism meaning "Hell." The implication being that, should a *Dung Si* betray any one of these sacred nine virtues, he will surely end up drinking the bitter waters from all nine springs believed to flow through Hell!

Dragon's Eyes and Hero's Heart

Long nhan literally means "Dragon's Eyes" and refers, first, to the attitude (*cach dien*) of the Cao Dai warrior and, second, a nickname Cao Dai warriors often used when referring to themselves, their individual and collective powers, and to their mission in life.

Faithfully following the nine virtues gave the Cao Dai warrior these *Long nhan*, the "Eyes of the Dragon."

More importantly, remaining true to this warrior code insured *Cao Dai Dung Si* warrior maintained *Anh Hon*, "The hero's heart," a euphemism for purity of spirit.

———

In the end, the Cao Dai warrior sought to live his life — no matter how brief — with the ideal of *Lam tho*, literally, "to compose a poem," living his life as if each day, each action, was a line in a great — heroic! — poem, a poem that would be sung by others — as an example to future generations of warriors — long after he had leapt into the Void!

Binh Co: "Strategy and Tactics"

Life is war. And war is divided into two parts: Strategy, our overall view of things, and tactics, specific techniques applied to specific situations.

Strategy can be likened to a general directing the movement of an army while standing on a mountain nearby. From his vantage point he can see "the Big Picture," the major movements of men and machinery and he can issue orders directing their deployment.

Keeping with this same scenario, tactics then are the individual clashes of individuals and groups of individuals taking place down on the battlefield. Each of these "little battles" must be fought with tactics specific to the terrain, the number of combatants involved, and a dozen other factors. Likewise, within each of these small battles, each fighter must decide what *techniques* to use at any given moment.

Thus the use of strategy and tactics, as well as specific techniques, is what makes up "the Art of War."

Within each of these three — Strategy, Tactics, Technique — are further choices that, in the West, are known as the "Direct Approach" and the "Indirect Approach."

Martial art, like life in general, comes down to a matter of simple choices.

Cheng versus Ch'i

In his masterwork *Ping Fa* (*The Art of War*), Sun Tzu tells us that when it comes to warfare, we have two approaches to choose from: *Cheng* and *Ch'i*, "direct force" and "indirect force."

Philosophically, we can also apply this choice to life in general: choosing to meet life "head-on" or to deal with the situations more "subtly." In the same way we can choose to meet an enemy force head-on, matching them blow for blow. Or we can meet them more obliquely, outmaneuvering them. This applies whether we are speaking of a major clash of armies or two warriors locked in a brutal one-on-one, life-or-death, unarmed struggle.

This classic *Cheng-Ch'i* choice is the bread and butter of guerilla fighters. It is suicidal for a smaller guerilla army to use *cheng* strategy and tactics, i.e., fighting toe-to-toe with a larger conventional army.

The Viet Cong knew this, having inherited their hit-and-run *ch'i* style of fighting from their fathers and grandfathers who had mastered the skill decades before fighting the French and the Japanese and then the French again.

On a personal combat level, it was difficult for lighter, shorter Asians to trade blow for blow with taller, more muscular Europeans.

The Viet Cong's main combat mandate was strategy, tactics and techniques conforming to a concept loosely translated into English as "cling to the belt." On the battlefield, this strategy meant that Viet Cong guerillas operated as far *inside* enemy "lines" as possible. During a firefight, this prevented American soldiers from calling in air strikes (for fear of hitting their own men).

During personal one-on-one combat, a smaller person is often *safer* "inside" (closer in) to a larger person since being closer in hinders the larger and taller person from striking with their longer arms (and/or kicks).

"Martial" Arts

First and foremost Cao Dai warriors remember that the word "martial" means "war." Thus the first purpose of *unarmed* martial arts is to compliment your war arsenal.

In a battlefield situation, *unarmed* martial arts is what you use in *between* weapons.

In a life-or-death struggle, the "art" part of "martial arts" takes a backseat to the "martial" part.

FYI: This is not to say there isn't a pure beautiful aesthetic to a perfectly performed *kata* (practice form). There is.

But all too often we hear a naïve novice claim they want to learn martial arts in order to "become one with the universe."

While peace is always the preferred option, war is all too often the *only* option. We are most at peace with the world when we feel we have nothing to fear from the world.

———

The essence of the "Art of War" is to upset your enemy's balance while safeguarding your own balance.

Having determined to "master" martial arts (the Art of War), we are then given the choice of how to proceed: *Quantity* versus *Quality*.

Some martial arts schools opt to teach their students as *many techniques* as possible, thus hoping to arm them against any eventuality they might find themselves confronted with.

Other martial arts schools teach only a *few techniques* . . . but they teach those few techniques extremely well, "drilling" those few techniques into students' heads until those techniques become second nature, until they become reflex, so that in a kill-or-be-killed situation the student will act on instinct. This is known as "the Boot-camp Approach."

Both of these approaches have their advantages. Both have flaws.

Learning a myriad of techniques does indeed arm a student with self-defense options, cutting down the odds that students might run up against a survival scenario not covered in only a "basic" course of self-defense.

On the other hand, mastering a *few* tried-and-true martial arts techniques, drilling them into us until we can do them in our sleep, means that, when faced with a life-or-death struggle, we will instantly react and that instant reaction will save our lives.

Fortunately, Cao Dai kung-fu students do not have to choose between these two approaches.

Cao Dai kung-fu teaches students a few *basic principles*, *natural* and universal methods of response and movement that can be applied to *any* survival situation.

Likewise, Cao Dai students are not asked to choose between *Cheng* or *Ch'i* responses, rather they learn to employ either or both responses as appropriate to each situation.

In the same way, Cao Dai kung-fu students are not asked to choose between what are generally called "hard" and "soft" styles of fighting.

Long Ho: The Dragon and The Tiger

Martial arts in general, and kung-fu styles in particular, are divided into "hard" and "soft" styles.

While these two overlap, in general, "hard" styles are so-called because they use direct, forceful (*Cheng*) techniques, the kind of forceful techniques people in the West generally identify with "karate."

"Soft" styles, on the other hand, use more oblique and indirect (*Ch'i*) methods of movement and striking we generally identify as "kung-fu." Thus, in "soft" style, rather than meet an attacker head on, "glancing" blocks and counterstrikes are used.

FYI: "Hard" styles of kung-fu have been traced back to a primitive Chinese art known as *Go-ti*, a form of no-holds-barred wrestling that included opponents goring one another with horned helmets!

"Soft" styles of kung-fu are usually traced back to a Taoist priest named *Chang San-feng* (1279–1368). Already a master of *Shao-lin Lo-han Chuan*, Chang had a dream one night in which God taught him how to fight. From this dream came the "soft" school(s) of kung-fu. (*Tai Chi: The Supreme Ultimate* by Lawrence Galante, 1981:19)

––––––––

Again, Cao Dai kung-fu students are not forced to choose between "hard" or "soft" schools of fighting since Cao Dai kung-fu freely "steals" tried-and-true fruits from both branches of the kung-fu tree of knowledge.

The Cao Dai criterion for adding *any* martial arts technique to their arsenal is simple: Does it work? Does it work *instantly?* And can a 98-pound woman use this technique to defeat an attacker twice her weight and half-again her size?

No matter how well-trained, no matter how physically fit a warrior (armored with muscle, etc.), there will be times when he is wounded (or, God forbid, *drunk!*) and that perfectly powerful punch he practiced while at his peak will fail him.

Thus, while the Cao Dai warrior knows he can use *muscular* force to "wrench" an enemy's arm into a lock/break, to perform that same arm lock *using only two fingers* and little or *no force*, means that particular technique will be one he can still use *when his own arm has been broken!*

––––––––

Attitude of attack also factors into any personal combat.

Again, to use the metaphor of life, as in personal combat, we can either "rush forward" (*Ap toi*) into combat, or else we can adopt an attitude of *An mon* and "wear down" an enemy's defenses.

Again we can see the advantage of smaller guerilla groups wisely choosing the latter approach.

In many ways, *An mon* strategy echoes the strategy of Miyamoto Musashi, who advises, in his 1643 samurai classic *A Book of Five*

Rings, what he describes as "Cutting at the edges," i.e., when you cannot overwhelm an opponent with a fierce direct (*Cheng*) attack, you attack his "fringe" with an indirect (*Ch'i*) attack.

In *Cao Dai Pha Do* this ploy is known as *Durong Vien*, attacking the edge/fringe.

———

For the Cao Dai warrior, the ultimate martial arts maxim is: If it works, use it and keep it! This is as it should be for any truly dedicated martial artist.

A personal story: On more than one occasion this author has had the privilege of studying with famed martial arts instructor Eddie Harris (presently operating out of Zanesville, Ohio).

A tough-nosed street fighter whose eclectic "School of Hard Knocks" fighting art testifies to his life-long love and pursuit of *all* martial arts, and to his familiarity with the harsh realities of both foreign and domestic battlefields, Master Harris was once asked by a reporter which, of all the styles he's mastered he favors when locked in a real-life, kill-or-be-killed struggle for survival.

"*Mo-Fo-Fu*," Master Harris replied.

Noting the confusion on the reporter's face, Master Harris explained with a wry smile, "When someone attacks me I just act like a *Mother Fuckin' Fool!*"

In other words: Whatever works.

Innovation and a constant updating of your art is the key. Never let tradition hold you back. Never let tradition get you killed!

Chapter Nine
Pha Do: Unarmed Combat

The Vietnamese term "Pha Do," pronounced "Fa Dough," literally means "to batter down," "to destroy," but is used generically to refer to all methods of unarmed combat, *Cao Dai Pha Do kung-fu* included.

Pha Do is sometimes used interchangeably with *Tac Chien*, "to fight."

As with most unarmed martial arts, study in Cao Dai Pha Do is composed of three phases: *tools*, *techniques*, and *targeting*.

"Tools" are those natural "weapons" we were born with (hands, feet, elbows, knees, teeth, etc.), tools we can easily hone to a sharper point.

"Techniques" are ways of using these tools Nature gave us, either to defend ourselves or else to cut down our enemies — often one and the same objective.

Finally, "targeting" means reaching a level of mastery where we can effectively wield the tools and techniques we have learned to protect ourselves and loved ones, and affect the plans of our enemy.

Mastering *Cao Dai Pha Do* requires our learning *Methods of Movement*, correct *Blocking*, *Striking* with hands, feet, and other bodily tools, *Grappling*, *Weapons Use*, and finally, familiarizing ourselves with *Shadow and Stealth* techniques; all tools and techniques we can use against our enemy, all tools and techniques our enemy is sure to try using against us!

Khuyen: Methods of Movement

Martial arts is 90 percent *positioning*. Attacked, we must instantly move ourselves "out of the line of fire" while simultaneously maneuvering into an advantageous position from which to effectively strike back into our opponent.

Where you are determines *how* you respond. For example, if you "shift" to the side, this "opens" different potential counterattack targets on your opponent's body than if you "squat" in and under his blow.

The Three Stances

How you stand also restricts your movement options. Despite all the elaborate posturing stances you see depicted in martial arts

Figure 7

The Three Stances

(1) Front ("Attack") Stance
(2) Back ("Rear") Stance
(3) Even ("Horse") Stance

movies, *physics* and common sense dictate that a fighter can only hold his weight in one of three stances:

(1) **Front Stance**: (aka "Attack Stance") With his weight distributed 70 percent on his forward/leading leg, 30 percent on his rear/tailing leg, your foe can only kick with his rear leg, since his weight restricts the movement of his forward leg.

(2) **Back Stance**: (aka "Defense Stance") With his weight distributed 70 percent on his rear leg and 30 percent on his front, your foe is able to kick with his leading leg only.

(3) **Even Stance**: (aka "Horse Stance") With his weight *evenly distributed*, he cannot kick with either leg until he shifts his weight one way or another, into a Front stance or a Back stance.

The Cao Dai fighter attacks the instant his opponent shifts into a "Horse Stance," knowing that his kicking ability will be restricted.

You can also attack when you see your opponent in a Front Stance (knowing that his lead leg is no danger to you).

Always move towards and attack into your foe's "full" leg, the leg that is carrying most of his weight.

In *Cao Dai Pha Do* stances are *Can Co* (literally the "root" and "foundation"). Undermining a castle's foundation is the first step in collapsing its defenses.

In Cao Dai Pha Do, *Khuyen* (literally "circle") refers to all methods of movement while fighting: advancing, retreating, ducking, etc. (See Figure 8.)

These *Methods of Movement* include the type of stance an opponent takes, "the Ten Directions of Movement," as well as methods of avoiding an attack while positioning yourself for counterattack.

The Ten Directions

It might seem that human beings have an unlimited choice when it comes to which direction to move. Were this true, there would be no way to correctly anticipate what direction our foe was about to move during a fight.

Fortunately, so far as fighting another human being is concerned, we are all restricted to *ten* directions of movement, corresponding to the eight directions on a compass, plus "down" (i.e., ducking/squatting) and "up" (leaping up, e.g., to avoid a sweep, etc.)

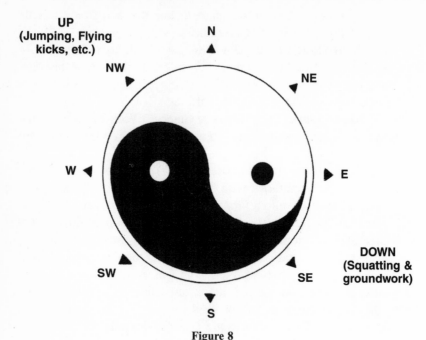

Figure 8
The Ten Directions of Movement

Thus, in a combat situation, we have the option of moving forward (either straight or diagonally), stepping back (either straight or diagonally), shifting side-to-side, ducking down out of the line of fire, or jumping up to avoid a low-level attack.

Take heart: These are also the options our foe is limited to.

Therefore, by watching his *stance*, we can foresee which direction a foe is about to shift.

This skill is best accomplished by our first becoming aware of our own stance and by how we *instinctually* move when threatened by certain dangers.

For example, when suddenly attacked by an overhead attack (e.g., attacked by a bludgeon) the natural human instinct is to crouch down and throw up our hands.

Rather than try to "program" some complex — unfamiliar — martial arts movement into a student, Cao Dai Pha Do instructors *build on natural reactions.* In this case, a student's natural "crouching/hands up" position is "sharpened" into an effective "High Block, Palm Strike" counterstrike. (See Figure 9.)

Figure 9
Natural reactions become martial arts techniques

Cao Dai Pha Do warriors step and shift along these ten basic lines of movement, shifting away from an attack, while positioning themselves for an effective counterstrike.

The Three Shifts

Faced with an enemy attacking from the front, rather than "backpedal," the Cao Dai warrior "shifts" (*Lang tranh*, literally "evade") out of the line of fire using one of the following movements:

(1) **Diagonal Shift**: Move forward at an angle to your foe's attacking arm or leg. Simultaneously, block his attacking arm with a "Cross-body Block" and counterattack into his "centerline."

Figure 10
Diagonal Shifting

(1) Blocking/deflecting your opponent's punching attack,
(2) Move forward by stepping either right or left diagonally.

(2) **Heel Shift**: (aka "Chinese Shift"). Without moving, twist/shift your weight onto your leg furthest from your attacker while turning your lead leg onto its heel, thus avoiding your foe's punch.

Augment this shift with a cross-body block and with a counter-strike into his centerline.

Figure 11
Heel Shift

(3) **Horse Shift**: As your foe attacks, pick up your leading leg and place it to the rear, to form a "Horse Stance." This movement cuts your "body profile" in half, making you a more difficult target to hit.

Do not "land" in your Horse Stance stiff-legged. Rather, land with legs "flexed" like springs. Use these "springs" of your landing to launch yourself into a counterstrike.

Half-Moon Stepping

When moving forward or to the rear, it might appear a Cao Dai warrior is moving straight forward or straight back but in reality they always step in a "Half-Moon" Step, slightly swinging the stepping leg in towards the other leg before setting it out into a firm stance.

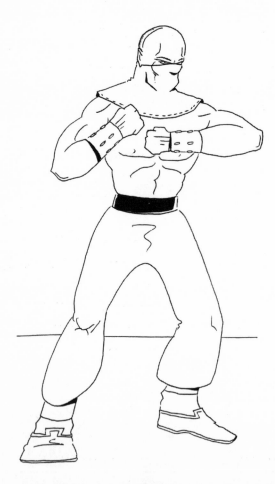

Figure 12
Half-Moon Stepping

Hidden within this Half-Moon Step is a take-down sweep, allowing you to shift/step outside an attacker's arm, before then sweeping back in to take your foe's leg out from under him with a leg sweep.

Figure 13
Half-Moon Takedown-Sweep

(1) Having closed with your attacker,
(2) Swing your leg closest to him out and back in (Half-Moon Step) sweeping his leading leg out from under him, toppling him to the ground.

"Crossing"

Another way to move into an advantageous position for counter-attacking your opponent is by "crossing" him.

When two fighters are facing one another, we call this being "boxed" (i.e., their shoulders squared with one another, your "Centerline" aligned with his). In this position, all your opponent's weapons (hands and feet) can easily reach you.

Figure 14
Fighters Boxed, i.e., standing toe-to-toe

Adopting a more side-oriented stance (i.e., one hand leading, one side more towards him) cuts down on the targets he can hit on you, but conversely takes some of your weapons further back (i.e., your trailing hand and foot).

Figure 15

Shifting Back

Shifting back into a more side-oriented stance makes you less of a target

(1) **Forward Crossing**: In order to achieve this side-stance positioning, we can take one step back, to form a "Back Stance" or "Horse Stance." (See Figure 7.)

Better yet, we can move *forward* into our attacker by "crossing" his "centerline."

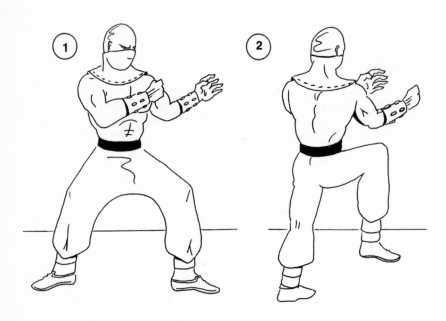

Figure 16
Crossing Forward

(1) Starting from a "Horse Stance,"
(2) Pick up your rear/trailing foot and place it down forward into an identical "Horse Stance."

As you move forward, *raise/fold your leading leg*. This both helps protect your groin and lower body from your foe's defensive strikes as you move towards him, while also preparing you to throw a kicking strike.

From this "cocked" position it is a simple matter of extending/ snapping your folded leg out into a "Thrusting Kick" or a "Crescent Kick."

Figure 17
Crossing Pivot

(1) Beginning in a "Horse Stance,"
(2) Pick up your rear/trailing foot, pivot (spin around) 180° forward, either placing your leading foot down into a combat stance or extending your forward leg into a kicking strike, e.g., and "Outside Crescent Kick." (See Figure 36.)

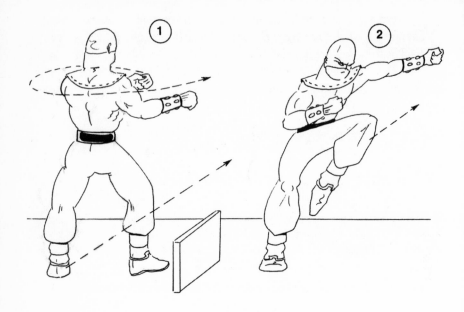

Figure 18
Over-the-Fence

(1) Picking up your rear/trailing foot, pivot forward 180°, as if stepping over a small fence or log,
(2) As you "clear" this "fence," lash out with a "Spinning Back Fist" strike and/or with an extended leg strike, e.g., a "Spinning Outside Crescent Kick." (See Figure 36.)

(2) *"Over-the-Fence."* A variation of "Crossing" requires picking up your rear/trailing leg and turning/pivoting 180° as you lash out with a "Spinning" *Back Fist* strike and/or with an *Outside Crescent Kick.*

While this move might at first appear "fancy" and daunting, it is as simple as raising your foot to "hop" over a short foot-high fence (hence its name).

———

While there are an endless number of combinations when it comes to moving into and away from an attacker, in the final analysis, there are actually only a few *Methods of Movement* that different schools of fighting combine in order to accomplish specific results.

Thus by mastering these "simple" *Methods of Movement* the *Cao Dai Pha Do* warrior is able to position himself so as to, first, evade his foe's assault, before then striking back into his foe with devastating results.

Cho Ang: Blocking

The first rule in Cao Dai Pha Do when it comes to blocking a foe's attack is: *There is no blocking!*

Faced with an attack, rather than first block and then counterstrike into a foe, Cao Dai Pha Do Warriors *strike into the offending limb.*

For example, faced with a punching attack, we can either first block the attacking arm and then counterstrike the attacker or, we can use our initial movement to strike into and perhaps cripple the attacking arm.

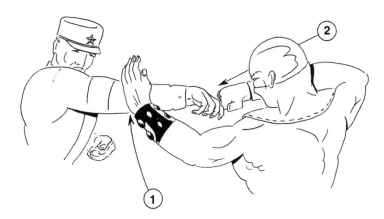

Figure 19
Counter-punching

(1) Rather than "waste time" blocking, counterattack into your opponent's attacking arm by striking into his elbow with a counterpunch or Palm Strike.

(2) To counter a grappling attack, punch into his extended fingers.

Cao Dai Pha Do warriors strike each blow as if that one blow is the only blow they will get.

This is not to say that every "block" thrown by a Cao Dai warrior is a forceful *Cheng* type "block" meant to break the attacking arm (or leg).

Cho Ang literally means "to drape a piece of cloth" over something. It can also mean "to smother," as in to smother out a fire, e.g., by covering it with a blanket.

Some Cao Dai Pha Do *Cho Ang* "blocks" come from the "soft" school of kung-fu, for example, the *Doc Xa* "Viper" block which doubles as a striking technique.

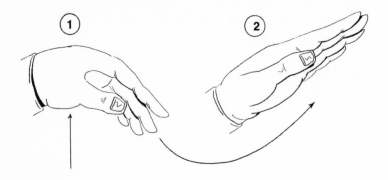

Figure 20
Doc Xa Viper Strike

(1) Striking into your opponent's attacking arm, damaging and deflecting it with a "Viper's Head" wrist block/strike (aka "Turtle's Head"),

(2) Use the "springboard" effect of your wrist blow to strike into your attacker's soft targets (e.g., throat, eyes) with thrusting fingers "Viper Strike."

Yet even when a "block" appears "soft" to the uninitiated, that "soft block" first stuns the foe by striking (i.e., "numbing") his blocked arm in preparation for a follow-up finishing strike.

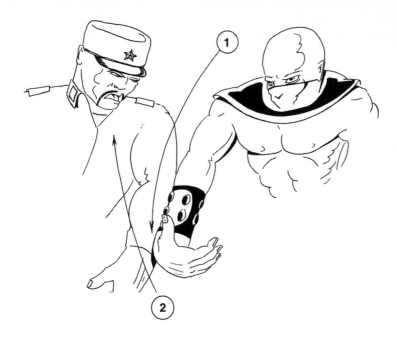

Figure 21
Soft Blocking

(1) As your attacker throws his punch, deflect his force with
    your wrist.
(2) Immediately upon deflecting his punch with your "soft"
    wrist block, "whip" your wrist up and around, striking him
    forcefully in the throat, face, etc., with a "Turtle's Head"
    wrist strike.

Cao Dai Pha Do "soft technique" teaches fighters that, if they
cannot strike into the attacking limb to cripple it, they can "glance
off" the attacking limb and use the power of the attacking limb to
augment and empower their own counterstrike.

For example, in the *Doc Xa* technique just mentioned, the blocking hand "gathers" additional energy when it uses the attacker's
blocked arm like a "diving board" to propel a counterstrike into the
attacker's face.

Likewise, a "*Palm-Up Block*" doubles as a "*Monkey-Paw Strike*" which, in turn, uses the foe's blocked arm as a "spring board" to launch a "Tiger-Claw Strike" into his face.

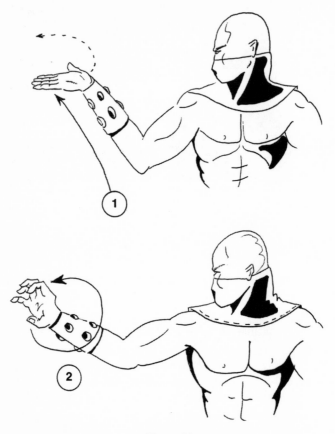

Figure 22
Palm-Up Block

(1) Use a "Palm-Up Block" to block-strike your opponent's attacking arm, and to strike into his throat when used as a "Monkey's-Paw Strike." (See Figure 30.)
(2) Having successfully blocked his attacking arm, use the "resistance" from striking his arm to "spring board" into a Tiger-Claw follow-up strike.

This same principle is used in kicking.

When a Cao Dai Pha Do practitioner uses a *Chinese Cross-Kick* to block/strike a low-level kick, he uses this same *Glancing Principle* to reroute his "blocking" leg into a Side Thrusting Kick.

Figure 23

Chinese Cross-Kick Combination

(1) Corkscrew your foot in to strike your opponent's knee.

(2) Use the rebounding "spring board" force of your initial strike to launch you into a "Side Thrusting Kick" *without* having to place your foot down.

Review: Blocking Rule #1: There are *no blocks* in Cao Dai Pha Do.

Blocking Rule #2: If it's below your waist, block it with your legs; above the waist, block it with your hands. Meaning: Block low-level kicking attacks and/or punches to your lower abdomen by raising your knees and legs.

Higher-level attacks (punches, kicks to the head) you naturally "block" with your hands.

Figure 24
The Waist Rule

(1) If an attack is aimed at targets above your waist, block it with your hands.

(2) If an attack is aimed at targets below your waist, block it with your legs.

Remember that you can also block/strike with your elbows.

Dung: Striking

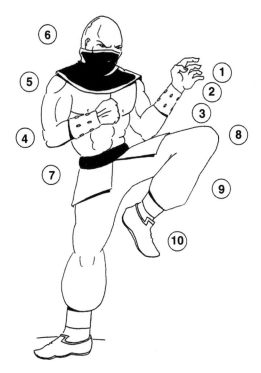

Figure 25

Your Kung-Fu Weapons

(1) *Hands* for blocking, striking, and grappling.

(2) *Wrists* for blocking and striking.

(3) *Forearms* for blocking and striking.

(4) *Elbows* for blocking and striking.

(5) *Shoulders* for striking.

(6) *The Head* for "butting," *teeth* for biting, *spitting* to distract and blind.

(7) *Hips* for striking into an opponent in order to unbalance and throw him. cf. jujutsu.

(8) *Knees* for striking and blocking.

(9) *Shins* for blocking, striking, and sweeping.

(10) *The Foot* for blocking, striking, and sweeping.

Having successfully positioned yourself "out of the line of fire," you can then strike back into your foe, ideally with a single, telling strike that will end the confrontation.

Recall that the Vietnamese term for martial arts, *Pha Do*, literally means "To batter down."

Other similar terms include: *Da*, *Ghe*, *Dot phe*, and the slang *Uc*, all of which mean to "strike."

Still other terms refer to specific kinds of striking, e.g, *Cu danh*, "blows and strikes," *Cung*, "to hit the head with the knuckles," and *Bop tai*, "striking the face."

The Vietnamese word *Dung* literally means "to collide with" and "to strike against," especially in a violent way.

Your options so far as to *where* and *how* to strike into your opponent will be limited only by your imagination.

Anything on your body (or in your hand for that matter; see "*Bat Am*: Combat with Weapons") can be used to strike into and disable your opponent.

Your choice of *Cu Danh*, "striking tools," will depend on time and clime, on where you are when facing what enemy. Every situation is different, therefore you must always be ready to adapt to flux and circumstance. But while every situation is different, a warrior's response is always the same . . . an *effective* one!

Factors such as your distance from an enemy ("The Gap"), whether he is wielding a weapon, whether you are dealing with more than one attacker, etc., all influence your response (e.g., a kicking response versus a punching response versus a grappling counter).

All your striking "tools" can be used to strike any number of targets on your opponent's body. These striking tools include hands, feet, and miscellaneous weapons such as elbows and knees, and head-butts.

Xich Thu: Hand Technique.

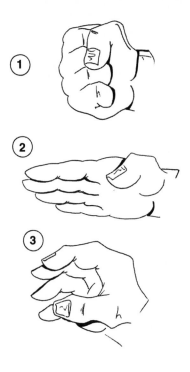

Figure 26
The Three Hands

(1) Closed Fist (aka "Hammer")
(2) Open Hand (aka "Sword," "Spear," "Monkey's Paw")
(3) Claw Hand (aka e.g., "Tiger's Claw")

The Vietnamese *Xich Thu* means "empty hand" and is similar to the Okinawan "Kara" (empty) and "te" (hand) from which we get *Karate*, literally "Empty hand."

Many kung-fu schools use purposely confusing hand positions, some as legitimate striking tools, some merely meant to identify the school and/or intimidate the unintitiated.

Don't let yourself be "psyched out" when faced with the prospect of learning these, or when finding yourself facing an opponent flashing these arcane hands at you.

All these various hand positions are actually *only three*:

- Closed Hand (Punching, knuckle fist, Back Fist Strike, Hammer Fist, etc.)
- Open Hand (Karate "chop," stabbing fingers "Spear Hand," "Monkey's Paw," etc.)
- Claw Hand (various fingers splayed, such as "Tiger's Claw," "Eagle's Claw," etc.)

In Cao Dai Pha Do, each of these *Xich Thu* can be used in a variety of ways to strike:

(1) *Bua:* **Hammer-fist**: The closed hand "fist" can be used to strike forward either in the Western "boxer's" style (striking with the full hand), or with the two-knuckle horizontal "karate" fist, or with the single knuckle vertical "Chinese" style fist.

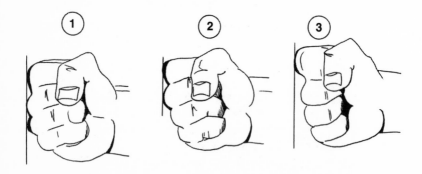

Figure 27
Fist Styles

(1) Western "Boxer's Fist" (full knuckles).
(2) "Karate Fist" (first two knuckles). Also Back-Fist, Hammer-Fist, etc.
(3) "Kung-Fu Fist" (striking with single knuckle) aka "Chinese Fist."

The Hammer Hand can also be used as a "bludgeon" to literally strike like a "hammer," smashing with the "beefy" edge of the hand. The closed hand can also be used as a "Back Fist."

Figure 28
Hammer-Strike and Back Fist

(1) The Closed Hand/Fist can be used like a "Hammer" to pound into various targets, e.g., the collarbone, bridge of the nose, the temple, etc.
(2) The Closed Hand can also be used as a Back Fist, striking with the back of the hand, first knuckle extended, against such targets as the temple.

(2) *Kiem:* **Blade Hand**: Kiem literally means "sword." Thus this hand position can be used both to "stab" into an enemy and also to "chop" down onto him like a hatchet (Vietnamese *Riu*).

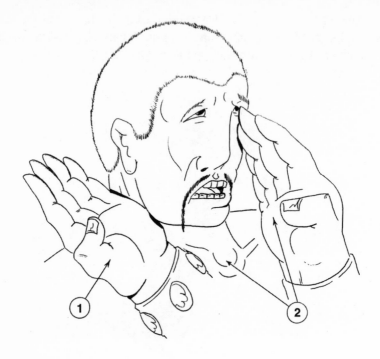

Figure 29
Open Hand Applications

(1) The Open Hand (aka "sword," "Axe") "chops" into an opponent, targeting the collarbone, throat, sides and back of the neck, etc.
(2) The Open Hand "Spear" can also be used to stab into "soft" targets, e.g., eyes, throat.

The Sword Hand has the advantage of being able to strike into "tighter" areas where a fist cannot go, for example, into an enemy's throat. This is accomplished by inverting the Sword Hand and striking with the "thumb forward" side in what is known as "The Monkey's Paw."

Figure 30
Monkey's Paw

(1) The "reverse" (thumb side) Sword Hand can be used to target the throat, temple, groin, etc.

The Sword Hand can also deliver more force to "hard" targets such as the ribs simply because its contact surface is smaller therefore its power is not as distributed as is a flatter fist. This allows the Sword Hand "chop" to slip in-between the ribs for maximum contact.

(3) ***Bira Cao:* Claw Hand**: *Bira Cao* means a claw, e.g., an animal claw. It can also mean "rake." *Urng*, meaning both "claw" and "talon," and *Mong vuot*, "claws," are sometimes used in place of *Bira Cao*.

All these terms are closely associated with *Xe*, "to tear," which is exactly what this kind of strike does.

In Chinese kung-fu, several styles specialize in clawing strikes, notably Dragon, Tiger, and Northern Eagle Claw styles.

In Vietnamese Pha Do, clawing strikes are both well-represented and respected.

Clawing attacks most often target "soft" tissues, e.g., throat, eyes, testicles and joint tendons, and can instantly cripple a foe.

Clawing strikes are often delivered from oblique striking angles which make it difficult if not impossible for a foe to block.

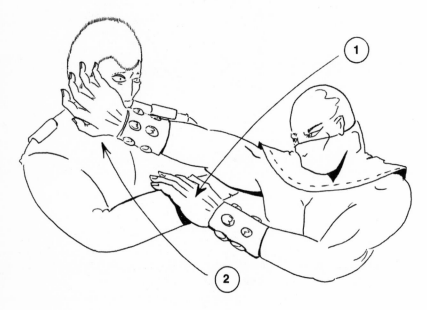

Figure 31
Oblique Tiger Claw Strike

(1) Shift to the *outside* of your attacker's punch while simultaneously "smothering" his attacking arm with a forceful Palm-Strike.

(2) Counterattack with an "Oblique Tiger Claw Strike" that attacks along an "oblique" horizontal path. Target his eyes and throat. *Note:* An "oblique" strike first crosses your attacker's "centerline" before then "reversing" direction to strike back into him.

Clawing attacks are often paired with other strikes. For example, a Descending Tiger Claw Strike involves first striking your foe with a Palm Strike before striking into him with your claw.

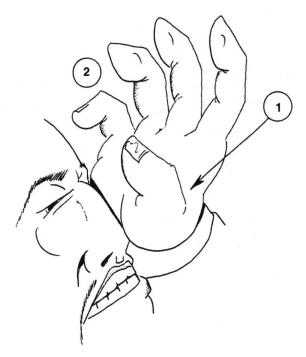

Figure 32
Tiger Claw/Palm Strike Combination

(1) Target the bridge of your attacker's nose with a Descending Palm Strike.
(2) Immediately upon connecting with your Palm Strike, "tighten" your hand into a Tiger Claw, attacking the "soft" tissues of his face. (See Figure 56.)

———

"In seeking, *know.* In knowing, *strike.* In striking, *strike well!* And in striking well, *accomplish all things.*" (Wan Tzu)

Doi: Kicking Technique

An attacking foe comes within striking range of our feet first, before we can reach him with our fists. Therefore, kicks are our first striking weapons.

Watching martial arts movies, one gets the impression there are *hundreds* of different martial arts kicks. While it is true there are an endless variety of ways to use kicks, there are actually *only four* types of kicks in all the martial arts. This is because anatomy and physics dictate that we can only extend our legs in one of four ways:

Figure 33
Front Kicks

(1) **Front Kicks** strike straight forward vertically by first raising your knee and then snapping or thrusting forward with the foot, striking with either the toe (when wearing hard shoes) or with the ball of the foot or the heel when barefoot.

(2) **Side Kicks:** Standing with your one side towards the enemy, raise ("fold") your forward leg and then thrust your leg towards your foe on a horizontal plane, striking with the flat of the foot, the heel, or the leading edge of the foot (aka "Swordfoot").

Figure 34
Side Kicks

(3) **Round Kicks** circle up and around from the floor on a horizontal plane as we rotate our hips forward.

There are two variations of Round Kick: the "Roundhouse," circling forward to strike with the toe, and the "Hook Kick," striking outwards to strike with the heel.

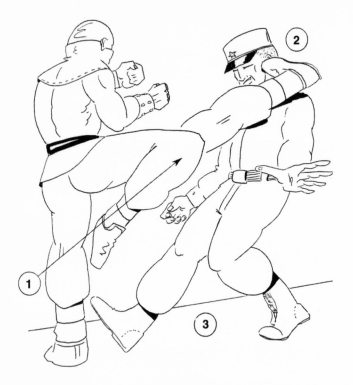

Figure 35A
Front Round Kick (aka "Roundhouse")

(1) Fold your knee as you raise your leg sharply and twist inwards, "rolling your hip."

(2) Reaching the extent of your stretch, suddenly snap your folded knee open, striking your target with your foot.

(3) Use this kick as a sweep by targeting your opponent's lower leg. *Note:* Strike with the instep or with the ball of your foot (toes bent back) when barefooted or when wearing soft-toed shoes. Strike with the toe of your foot when wearing hard-toed shoes.

Figure 35B
Reverse Round Kick (aka "Hook Kick")

(1) Facing off with your opponent, simultaneously raise and fold
your leading leg. Reaching the apex of your stretch, suddenly
release your folded leg, whipping it into your opponent along
a horizontal path to strike with your heel.

(4) **Arcing Kicks** circle up and around vertically, drawing an "arc"
in the air as they strike either outwards (away from your body) or
inwards (in towards your "centerline"). Also known as "Crescents"

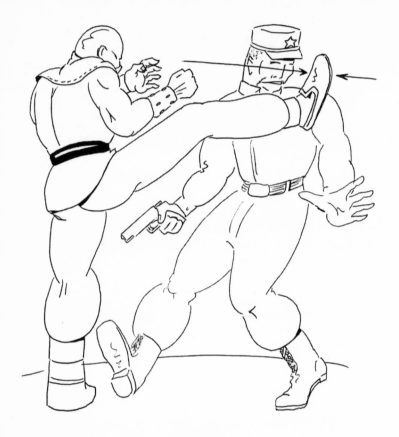

Figure 36
Arcing Crescent Kick

and "Axe Kicks," these kicks strike with the outside and inside edges of the foot.

All martial arts kicks, both "hard" school and "soft" school, can be classified into one of these four categories.

While there are only four kicks, the use of these four basic kicks is limited only by the imagination and determination of the individual warrior.

For example, these four basic kicks easily become *dozens of kicks* when combined with *Methods of Movement* such as "Over-the-

Fence" (see Figure 18) and with jumping, as favored by such schools as Korean Tae-Kwon do and Okinawan shotokan karate.

FYI: Some Cao Dai *Quang Boi* fighting cadres are known — and feared! — for their mastery of kicking techniques, although the *ideal* is for the Cao Dai warrior to be balanced in his martial arts, not favoring hand over foot, nor any particular technique or style, so as not to become predictable.

Predictable = dead!

"Gan chua goi but banh anh!" the Cao Dai say, i.e., "Familiarity breeds contempt" . . . and also death!

———

Kicking techniques and other forms of striking go hand-in-hand. For example, a basic *Pha Do* "run" (attack combination) uses both hand strikes and feet kicking. (See Figures 37 and 38.)

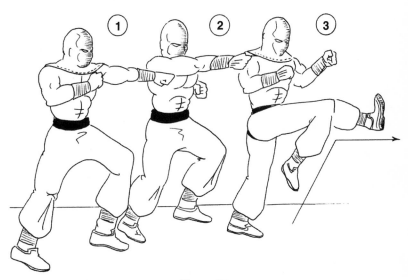

Figure 37
Pha Do Attack Combination I

(1) Leading Punch
(2) Reverse Punch
(3) Kick

Figure 38

Pha Do Attack Combination II

(1) Kick
(2) Leading Punch (Always land with a hand!)
(3) Reverse Punch

There are two rules to remember when adding kicks to your *Pha Do* arsenal.

First: *Always land with a hand*. Having connected a solid kick to your enemy, don't step back to "admire your work," rather, use the momentum of your "landing" (i.e., placing your kicking foot down) to strike into your already stunned foe with a hand strike designed to finish him off.

Correct hand striking form + the momentum of your "landing" = additional power to your finishing strike.

The second rule for kicking is *kick on the break*. When pushing away from a grappling attacker, always kick as you separate, as this is when a fighter is most likely to drop his guard.

Professional kickboxers call this "kicking on the break" and formidable footboxers such as Thai kickboxers and French *Savate* fighters are notorious for this tactic.

Also when grappling, Cao Dai warriors often employ the "Scorpion" technique: seizing hold of an opponent's arms while smashing his legs and lower body with savage kicks (in the same way a scorpion grabs its prey with its claws before striking with its deadly tail).

FYI: In his *Ping Fa*, Sun Tzu refers to a similar tactic which he calls the "Twice Striking Snake," i.e., when you attack the snake's head, its tail strikes you; grabbing for its tail, you are struck down by its fangs.

Cao Dai often call martial arts kicking techniques *Ngura chien,* "War horse," meaning your kicks should be as hard as those of a veteran war horse.

A skilled kicker earns the nickname *Ran-ret,* "centipede" (a hundred legs, get it?), or the less flattering — but no less deadly! — *La,* someone who kicks like a "mule."

FYI: The French martial art/sport of *Savate* (French "Old Shoe"), formalized around 1862, owes much to Vietnamese martial arts. French sailors and later French colonists took foot-fighting techniques back to France from Asia. To give everyone their due, French fighters and freebooters undoubtedly gleaned foot-fighting techniques from many Asian ports-of-call, including Thailand, and from the Chinese.

Vietnamese kung-fu also undoubtedly influenced the creation of the Brazilian martial art *Coperia,* reportedly brought to South America by sailors and slaves. (See *X-Treme Boxing: Secrets of the Savage Street Boxer,* by Christopher B. Prowant, Paladin Press, 2002.)

Major trading centers such as Saigon and Hanoi, as well as trading spots up and down the coast of Vietnam, regularly hosted foreign visitors, so there is no way of knowing for certain how many other martial arts in Asia and throughout the world were influenced by Vietnamese kung-fu.

Additional Striking Tools

Any hard — bony — part of your body can be used to strike your opponent:

(1) *"Turtle's Head."* The wrist (*co tay*) is an oft overlooked striking weapon in many martial arts, but not in Cao Dai Pha Do. This hard surface (called *Tranh*) is the best example of a "blocking" tool that is really a "striking" tool.

In Chinese *wu-shu*, this striking with the wrist is part of the "Crane" style of fighting.

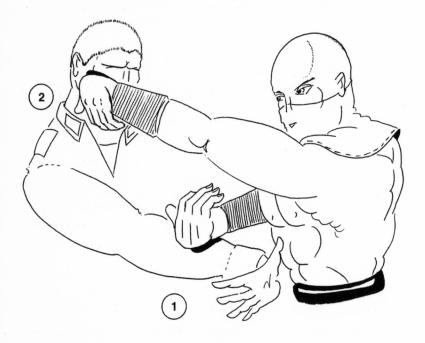

Figure 39
Co Tay Turtle's Head Striking

(1) Use a cross-body Turtle's Head to block/strike your attacker's arm.
(2) Simultaneously counterattack into your opponent with a second Turtle's Head Strike, targeting his temple and jaw line.

(2) The **Forearm** can be used to both strike and to strangle.

As a striking tool, the forearm can be used to "clothesline" a foe (i.e., striking into his face with your extended forearm).

The forearm is also the primary tool used for strangling an enemy and/or for striking up into his throat. (See "*Tri Thu*: Grappling".)

The infamous *Thuggee* strangler cult of India were masters of using the forearms as an offensive weapon. (See *The Ancient Art of Strangulation*, by Dr. Haha Lung, Paladin Press, 1995.)

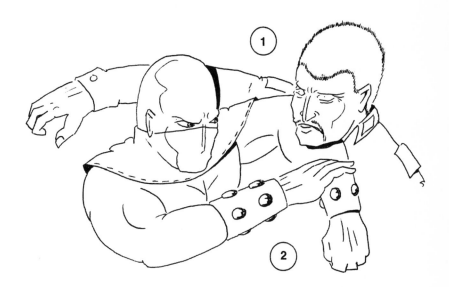

Figure 40
Forearm Use

(1) Strike into an attacker's face and throat with your forearm.
(2) The forearm can also be used to strangle an opponent and/or crush his larynx. *Note:* Forearm techniques should be augmented by "pinning" your opponent against a wall, etc.

(3) "**Shortwing**" elbows (*Khuyu tay*) are excellent "close-in" striking tools. Elbows also have the advantage of allowing a smaller person or a lighter woman (who might be unable to deliver a strong punch) to deliver a devastating blow to a larger opponent.

Cao Dai fighters call the elbow *Canh*, meaning, "wing," or sometimes Canh chuon, "Dragonfly's wing."

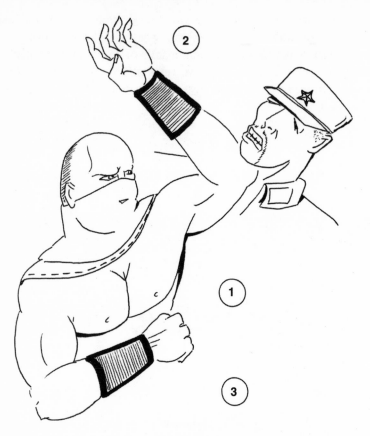

Figure 41
Khuyu tay Elbow Technique

(1) Rising Elbow Strike
(2) Descending Elbow Strike
(3) Horizontal "circling-in" Elbow Strike

(4) **Shoulder** strikes (*Bo*, literally "Ox") can be used to unbalance and/or knock the breath out of an opponent (when targeting the solar plexus).

Musashi, in his *A Book of Five Rings*, describes a samurai technique of repeatedly striking an opponent with the shoulder, hard enough to *kill*.

American football players have long known the shoulder technique to be useful.

(5) **Head-butts** can stun, render unconscious, and even kill an attacker. Called *Giac* by Cao Dai fighters (literally "Rhino's horn"), head-butts can be delivered forward, when locked in face-to-face combat, or backwards, when seized from behind by an attacker.

The viability of the head as a striking tool is shown by Okinawan *karateka* breaking boards, ice, and even bricks with their head.

In Ethiopia, the martial art/sport of *Reisy* is known for finishing confrontations with head-butts. (Prowant & Skinner, 2002.)

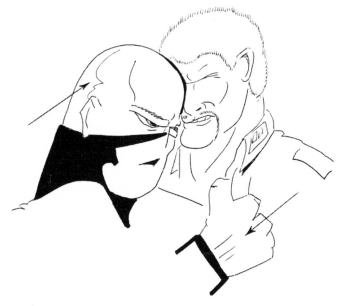

Figure 42
Headbutting

(6) **Hips** are invaluable weapons in the fighting art of *jujutsu* and in the sport it spawned, *judo*.

Not only can your hip be used to strike a painful blow into an opponent's hip and/or groin, the resultant collision unbalances your opponent, leaving him in a vulnerable position for a takedown/throw. (See "*Tri Thu*: Grappling.")

(7) **Knees** are one of the primary weapons of Thai kickboxers. Knees can attack on a horizontal plane (like a "Round Kick") and as a rising weapon targeting his groin and/or his face when pulled within striking distance.

Figure 43
Use of Knees

(1) Knees can be used to strike upwards into the groin, abdomen, and head.
(2) Augment knee strikes to the head by pulling your opponent's head down into your rising knee strike.

(8) Striking with the **Shin** is usually reserved for professional kickboxers who don't mind spending years desensitizing (and deforming) their shins by beating them against immovable objects.

For the rest of us, the hard shin can be used to sweep/strike into the soft calf muscle at the back of an opponent's leg, toppling him to the ground where other striking tools, e.g., heel/stomp, can then be brought to bear.

Figure 44
Shin Strikes

These additional striking weapons are often used in concert with one another. (See "*Bo Ten*: the Collapsing Principle.")

Co The Hoc: Where to Strike

"The more you know about the human body the easier it is to take it apart." (Skinner, 1995:41)

Every human body contains the same vulnerabilities.

Mastery of *Co the hoc* (anatomy) is a required course of Cao Dai warriors, not only in order to better take apart their foes, but also to better be able to put themselves and their comrades back together when need be.

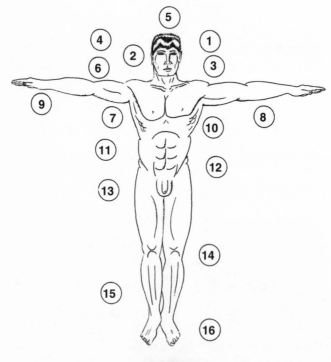

Figure 45A
Targets/Front

(1) Eyes: Attack with finger stabs and with "blinders" (e.g., powders, liquids, dirt, bright lights, sudden darkness, etc.).

(2) Ears: Attack with slender stabbing weapons (e.g., icepick) and with slapping Palm Strikes designed to disorient and unbalance. (See Figure 75.)

(3) Nose: Attack with sharp blows and with powders and liquids that interfere with his breathing.

(4) Temple: Attack with sharp blows (e.g., Back Fist Knuckle strike).

(5) Head: In general, the head can be attacked with bludgeons and with solid unarmed strikes.

(6) Neck and Throat: Target with bladed weapons and with solid unarmed strikes (e.g., Sword Hand Strikes directed against the front of the throat and the back of the neck).

(7) Clavicles: Target these "collarbones" with heavy bludgeons and with unarmed blows such as the Sword Hand and Hammerfist.

(8) Arms: Attack with heavy bludgeon blows, with Open Hand "chops" and with locking/breaking traps that target the elbow. (See Figure 63.)

(9) Wrists and Hands: Attack with solid blows (to break) and with wrenching "wrist-locks" and "finger-cranks." (See Figure 62.)

(10) Armpits: Strike up into this "soft" target with bladed weapons and with stiff-fingered jabs.

(11) Solar Plexus: Attack with solid blows and with stabbing weapons (i.e., bladed weapons and/or "Spear Hand").

(12) Abdomen: Attack with solid blows (hand strikes and kicks) and with stabbing weapons, armed and unarmed.

(13) Groin: Attack with strikes, with grabbing twists (to testicles), and with stabbing weapons.

(14) Knees: Attack with kicks designed to destroy the knee and with "locks" designed to unbalance your enemy. (See Figure 70.)

(15) Shins: Strike with bludgeons (e.g., *Bo*-staff), with painful blows, and with sweeping kicks. (See Figure 44.)

(16) Feet: Attack with stomps, and with painful twists when grappling.

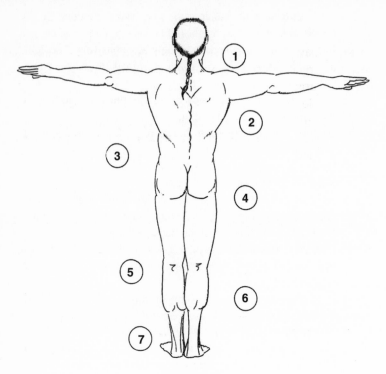

Figure 45B
Targets/Back

(1) Back of Head: Attack with blows targeting the juncture of the head and the neck (i.e., Atlas and Axis).

(2) Spine: Strike anywhere along the length of the "backbone" with blows and with blade stabs.

(3) Kidneys: Strike up into the kidney area with forceful blows and with blade stabs.

(4) Groin: Strike up into the groin from behind. (See Figure 74.)

(5) Back of the Knee: Stomping and sweeping into the back of the knee is an effective takedown technique.

(6) Calf: Damaging the calf with a forceful shin strike/sweep upsets his balance and restricts your opponent's movement.

(7) Achilles' Tendon: Damaging the Achilles' Tendon (with a stomp, sweep, etc.) upsets his balance and restricts his ability to maneuver.

Xung Ham: How to Strike

Once we have learned the striking weapons available to us, and learned the targets, *Xung ham*, we must then learn how to effectively strike those targets.

For example, while a Sword hand "chop" striking down onto a foe's clavicle (collarbone) can disable a foe, this kind of open-hand blow is twice as effective when you strike forward with your hand tightly clenched, snapping it open only at the last instant before impact.

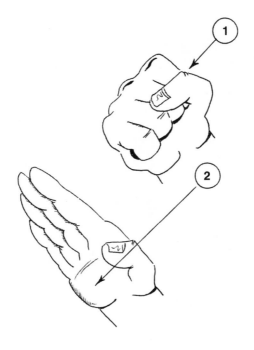

Figure 46
Close-to-Open Strike

(1) Striking *forward* with your Closed Hand,
(2) "Snap" your hand open an instant before connecting, "exploding" your energy into the target.

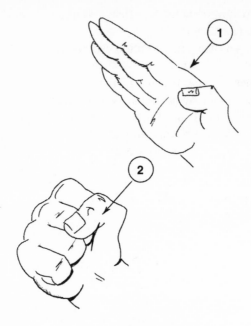

Figure 47
Open-to-Close Strike

(1) Striking forward with an Open Hand,
(2) "Snap" your hand closed, hardening your fist an instant
     before connecting with your target.

Conversely, when striking with a Hammer-Fist, slice your open
hand towards your target, closing your hand tightly an instant before
impact.

Yes, this takes timing and timing comes only through diligent
practice. But the "sweat equity" you must invest to master this skill
pays off in the long run since this method of striking increases the
impact of your strikes dramatically.

This same "Snapping Principle" is used when striking with a
Back-Fist Strike.

Instead of "leaning your weight into" your Back-Fist strike,
smoothly "snap" your Back-Fist the same way you snap a wet "rat-
tail" towel. In other words, close your open hand into a tight fist an

instant before making contact, in effect "whipping" your knuckles into your target. (See Figure 28.)

Cao Dai call this snapping motion *Noc ong*, "the sting of the wasp."

There are other "Rules of Striking" that will help maximize both your striking speed and the power of your striking.

The Four Directions of Striking

Striking attacks travel in only four directions. This applies to hand strikes, kicks, and weapons such as elbows and knees:

(1) **Straight forward** punches and kicks.

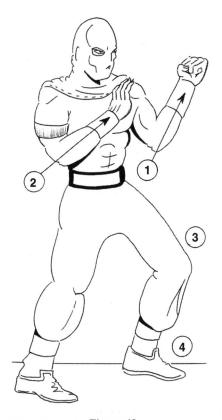

Figure 48
Straight-in-Striking

(2) **Rising** strikes, "Uppercuts," such as rising punches, vertical elbow and knee strikes, and rising kicks.

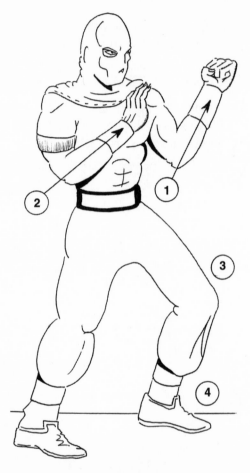

Figure 49
Rising Strikes

(1) "Uppercut" Punch.
(2) Rising "Palm-Strike."
(3) Rising Knee Strikes (See Figure 43).
(4) Rising Kicks (e.g., Front Snap Kick).

(3) **Descending** strikes, e.g., karate "chops," Hammerfist blows, and "Axe Kicks" that arc upwards before dropping onto a target. (See Figure 36.)

Figure 50
Descending Strikes

(1) Hand Blows (e.g., Hammer, Sword Strikes).
(2) Descending Elbow Strikes. (See Figure 85.)
(3) Drop onto a downed foe with a knee strike. (See Figure 76.)
(4) Stomping down kicks (e.g., targeting knee, finishing an already downed opponent).

(4) **Hooking-in** strikes, for example, a boxer's "Right Hook" punch, horizontal elbow strikes, "Round Kicks," sweeps, and horizontal knee strikes.

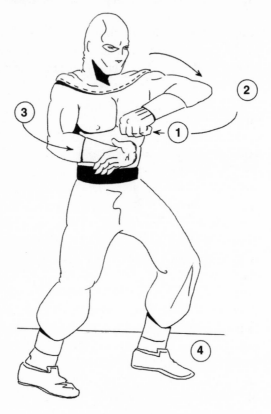

Figure 51
Hooking-in Strikes

(1) "The Hook" punch is a standard for both Western boxing and for Eastern Martial Arts.
(2) Elbows can be "hooked-in" as effective short-range weapons.
(3) Palm strikes, Spear Hand Strikes, and other kung-fu blows can be "hooked-in" as "body shots" targeting ribs, solar plexus, etc.
(4) Kicks such as the "Roundhouse" and "Hook" also "hook" into their targets. (See Figure 35.)

Specialized Blows

Some martial arts cadres are masters of unique forms of striking, specialized angles of attack, and telling blows designed to instantly incapacitate — or kill — an enemy:

(1) **Secrets of the Shadowhand**. "It is always best to avoid confrontation. However, when combat is unavoidable it is preferable to strike a foe from behind or from an oblique, unexpected angle. Confronting a foe face to face, it is best to strike such sure and sudden blows, one should then escape the scene as quickly as possible." (Lung and Prowant, 2000:15)

In warfare, the more you can disguise your intent and angle of attack, the better your chances of first befuddling, battering down, and then burying your enemy.

Japanese ninja call this *Taisavaki*, a strategy of fighting composed of the tactics and techniques of *Inno-jutsu* and *Inton-jutsu*, "Hiding" and "Escape and Evasion" respectively.

Cao Dai call such strategy *O Nha*, "Black Crow Technique," since its purpose is to cover your intent as if hiding it behind a crow's opaque obsidian wing.

Tactics of the *O Nha* sort are also sometimes called *Tan Cong Phu*, "Secondary attack," their intent being the use of a diversionary movement designed to distract your enemy from your actual intent:

"If my enemy does not know where I intend to attack, he must prepare everywhere. Preparing everywhere, he is strong nowhere." (Sun Tzu)

For example, in Figure 16, you move forward, "crossing" over your attacker's "centerline" with a sweeping-in attack while disguising your true intent: better positioning yourself for striking back into his body.

Likewise, in Figure 49, your initial Palm-Strike forces your foe's head up and back, preventing him from seeing your Rising Knee Strike.

The criteria for "Black Crow/Shadowhand" maneuvers and strikes are, first and foremost, that the action disguises us (our array of force, our intent, our plan and path of attack). We accomplish this by misdirecting our foe's attention, but striking him suddenly where least expected, and then escaping unscathed. (Lung and Prowant 2000:16)

(2) *Don Tri Mang:* **The Death Blow**. In Cao Dai kung-fu you deliver each strike as if it is the *only* strike you will get. If you succeed in raining a half dozen blows down onto your opponent, great! However, deliver each of those six blows as if it is *the only one* you will be able to hit him with.

Vietnamese call this type of purposeful striking *Cu Danh nga*, "the Knock-out blow" or, more ominously, "the Death Blow."

FYI: Gichin Funakoshi, the "Father" of modern karate, made his students internalize the concept of *Ikken Hisatsu*, literally, "To kill with one blow," i.e., to finish a fight quickly and decisively with a single blow — whether a masterful mental stroke of genius, or the slash of an equally keen metal blade.

(3) **The Poison Hand**. When a Cao Dai warrior mixes the "Form + Speed = Power!" formula with the *Cu Danh nga* attitude of striking, the result is their hitting an opponent so fast with so many blows that to the uninitiated it often looked as if the Cao Dai warrior had defeated his enemy with a single strike — a "Death Touch."

FYI: Stories of the dreaded *Dim Mak* (Chinese "Death Touch") are the stuff of legend throughout Asia, the object of endless quests by both dedicated martial artists and by any number of shadowy cadres.

While it is true a few gifted masters skilled in anatomy and Chi flow have ways of interrupting the natural flow of blood in the human body by stimulating or stifling specific acupuncture meridians (flow lines), theoretically causing illness, paralysis and even death, such deadly technique is — thankfully! — beyond the mastery of most people:

"While originally based on an in-depth and intricate study and careful mastery of human anatomy, techniques of the Death Touch were to eventually degenerate and find themselves replaced with ingenious and often elaborate methods of assassination which served the dual purpose of removing foes while at the same time perpetuating the myth that Ninja could kill with a glance, a word, a touch, or even strike down a foe from a distance or in securely locked rooms." (Lung, 1997 B:63)

Lacking the wherewithal to defeat a foe with bludgeon or blade, you can always bury him beneath a steaming pile of bullshit!

Thus, when a foe cannot be defeated face-to-face, subterfuge must be the order of the day. In days past, this often included martial arts schools "faking" possession of "the Death Touch." (See *"Ah Hiem."*)

Unscrupulous fighters sometimes dipped their fingers in poisons prior to a fight. During the fight, these poisons were secretly slipped into the other fighter's water, or secretly administered to him through touching, small needles, and some other medium. These poisons slowed his response time and/or killed him outright, making it appear he had succumbed to the "Delayed Death Touch" or a "Poison Hand" blow.

Since autopsies were unheard of until recent times, there was little chance such skullduggery would be discovered.

FYI: Modern day streetfighters often dip their fingers into bleach, hot sauce, or any toxic substance that can then be thrust into an opposing fighter's eyes, nose and mouth during a no-holds-barred fight.

———

As already mentioned, Cao Dai fighters were able to hit an opponent so fast with so many blows that it appeared they knew some "magical" means of killing with a single blow.

What the Cao Dai warriors were using was "the Collapsing Principle."

Bo Ten: The Collapsing Principle

Bo Ten is a Vietnamese word meaning a "sheaf of arrows." In Cao Dai Pha Do, *Bo Ten* refers to striking a foe rapid-fire and repeatedly, as if unloading a full quiver of arrows, one right after the other.

Some fighters use the slang *Xam* and *Van Than*, both of which mean "tattoo," to refer to striking a foe many times in rapid succession.

In English, this is called "the Collapsing Principle" after the way, instead of withdrawing, we "collapse" our initial strike into an immediate follow-up strike(s).

For example, having made "contact" with the enemy, rather than withdraw ("re-chamber") the attacking arm (like a boxer), the Cao Dai warrior "collapses" into his enemy, collapsing his Spear-Hand Strike into a punch, likewise collapsing his punch into a *Canh chuon* "Dragonfly" Elbow Strike. Thus we are able to strike our enemy with a rapid-fire "three-piece" in the time it would normally take a more traditional fighter to rechamber his fist for a second punch.

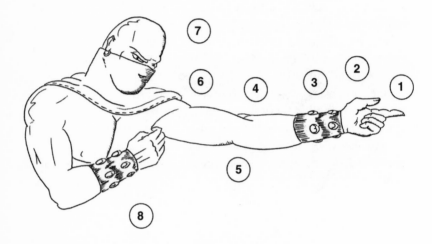

Figure 52
The Collapsing Principle

(1) Finger Thrust (e.g., Spear Hand) collapses into . . .
(2) Claw-Hand Strike and/or Knuckle Strike collapses into . . .
(3) "Turtle's Head" Wrist Strike collapses into . . .
(4) Forearm Strike collapses into . . .
(5) Elbow Strike collapses into . . .
(6) Shoulder Strike collapses into . . .
(7) Headbutt (and biting and spitting!) collapses into . . .
(8) Kicks and Grappling technique.

Once the idea of "the Collapsing Principle" is understood, striking technique can easily be paired with grappling technique. (See Figure 53.)

Figure 53
Collapsing Principle Takedown

(1) Squatting in under your opponent's attacking arm, smash into his solar plexus/ribs with a solid elbow strike.

(2) Your striking arm *stays in contact with his body* as it slides down his body to lock out his knee.

(3) Simultaneously, your other hand goes behind his calf to scoop his "locked-out" leg out from under him, toppling him to the ground. *Note:* Keep hold of your downed attacker's lock-out leg until you finish him off. (See Figure 76.)

Explosive Speed and Power

"Once the threat is upon us, once the wolves are at the door and the beast is at our throat, there is no time to fear, only time to react." (Skinner, 1995:10)

Mastering a martial arts technique begins with learning to correctly perform that movement — precisely — and this requires first learning the correct form.

"Practice" *does not* "make perfect" if we are taught to practice a movement incorrectly in the first place by not being shown — and held to — the *correct form*.

Correct form can be likened to digging an irrigation ditch: We first map out that ditch, then through repetitious digging we slowly carve out that ditch.

Having correctly surveyed and then dug our ditch, once we loose the flood waters, they will easily follow the deep ditch we've dug. Unimpeded, the water will flow down this ditch, *picking up speed* as it goes.

Should anything or anyone have the misfortune of getting in the way of this speeding wall of water, it will be crushed by the power of the rushing torrent.

In the same way, we train our muscles (and mind) to "flow" along a path of action. Then, when the wolf is suddenly upon us, without impeding thought (i.e., "panic" and "confusion"), our trained muscles respond without conscious thought and command from the "slower" brain.

Thus: Form + Speed = Power.

It works something like this: Ever accidentally scald your hand under a hot water faucet? Recall how you jerked your hand out from under the scalding water before you even had time to feel the pain, *before your brain even had time to register and respond to the pain signal!*

This is because the sensors in your scalded hand send signals to your brain and then "wait" for your brain to send "pain" signals back.

But, that signal must first pass through your spinal cord (which

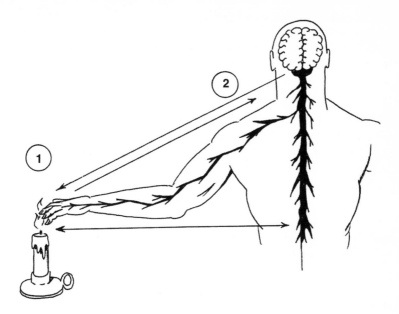

Figure 54
Body-Brain Response Time

(1) Encountering a "painful" stimulus, the nerves in your hand
    send a frantic signal rushing up the arm to the brain.
(2) On its way to the brain, this signal passes through the spinal
    cord which immediately sends a "Move!" command racing
    back down the muscles of the arm, *before* the initial mes-
    sage can even reach the brain.

controls your physical functions). As soon as the pain signal reached
the spinal cord, your body pulled back from the scalding water.

This is done *without conscious command* of the brain.

This is proof it is possible for you to move *faster than pain!*

It is just this *chieu anh* "reflex" that the Cao Dai warrior strives
to cultivate.

Cao Dai Pha Do defensive/offensive strikes and counterstrikes are crafted from *natural reactions*, e.g., instinctively throwing up our hands to protect ourselves when attacked.

Through repeated practice we train our body to react even before our mind can factor in all the input.

In a kill-or-be-killed situation our "fight or flight" instinct kicks in and we either run away from danger (always a respected option for the guerilla fighter!) or else we instinctively strike out at the attacking force.

In an offensive situation, we must train ourselves to "release" our body to do what it has been trained to do. This is called *X'ot*, swooping onto our prey like an eagle. Some martial arts schools refer to this as "Bridging the gap" between you and an opponent.

FYI: Karate schools teach students to yell a "Kiai!" (Japanese "Spirit shout") when striking, not only to "terrorize" their opponent, but also because screaming like a banshee helps "free up" the mind which, in turn, "releases" the trained body to do what it has been taught to do.

(1) **Increasing Speed**. The key to adding speed to our martial arts technique is to "program" reactions into our muscles (and mind) that kick in automatically when we are threatened.

As already mentioned, the best martial arts techniques are built on *natural reactions*, e.g., the natural reaction of throwing up our arms to block something coming at our face is easily "re-programmed" into an effective "X-Block."

In turn, successfully "X-Blocking" an attack positions us for an effective counterstrike.

Figure 55
Increasing Speed/Natural Reactions

(1) Using the *natural reaction* of "throwing up your hands" to block a punch to your head, block the attack with a "Cross-Block." (See Figure 78.)

(2) Catching his attacking arm in your Cross-Block, immediately pivot your leading leg back as you seize a hold of your attacker's arm, pulling your attacker's arm around and down. Augment this technique by smashing your elbow into his extended elbow. (See Figure 63.)

Likewise, the natural reaction of catching an apple thrown at your face is identical to the movements of "blocking" a punch to the face and countering with a Tiger-Claw strike.

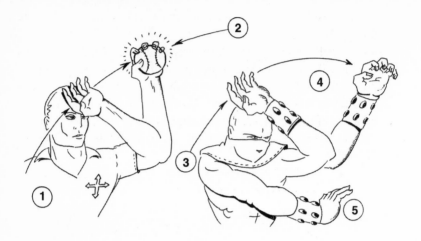

Figure 56
Natural Reactions/Tiger-Claw

(1) Perceiving a baseball or similar object flying towards your face, your hand *instinctively* comes up to protect your face.
(2) As you catch the ball, *your hand instinctively grasps* the ball.
(3) Faced with an attack (e.g., punch) to your head, your hand *instinctively* flies up to protect your face, sweeping aside the attacking hand.
(4) Your blocking hand continues to arch inwards, striking your attacker's face with a Descending Tiger-Claw Strike that *instinctively "grasps"* (and *tears!*) at your attacker's face in the same way your hand previously seized hold of the baseball. (See Figure 32.)
(5) See Figures 9 and 87.

(2) **Increasing Power**. Remember: Form + Speed = Power!
Use the following "Nine-Point Striking Form" to increase your striking power. (See Figure 57A-H.)
This exercise should be performed slowly and forcefully, keeping your arms, shoulders (deltoids), and side muscles (latissimus dorsi) "tensed" throughout. This kind of "dynamic tension" not only increases your muscle strength but will also help you "lock" these movements into your "muscle-memory" faster.

As you "push" your hands outwards (striking), breathe out slowly and forcefully.

As you "pull" your arms back in, breathe in, deep and slow — as if smelling a flower. Feel your lungs expand from the bottom up.

While performing this form, note how the various strikes naturally "collapse" into one another, allowing you to strike one blow immediately after the other, e.g., Straight Punch "collapses" into a vertical Back-Fist Strike; Upper-cut "collapses" into a "Snake-Punch."

Figure 57A and B

Nine-Point Striking Form

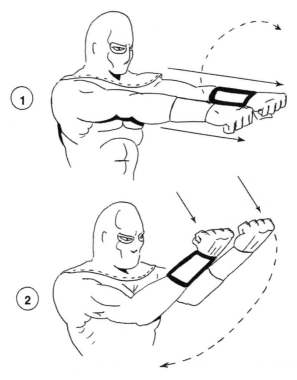

(1) Standing in a "Horse Stance," fists turned palms-up at the side of your chest, perform *Double Straight Punches*.
(2) Pulling your extended fists back in towards your chest, strike forward with *Descending Back-Fist Strikes*.

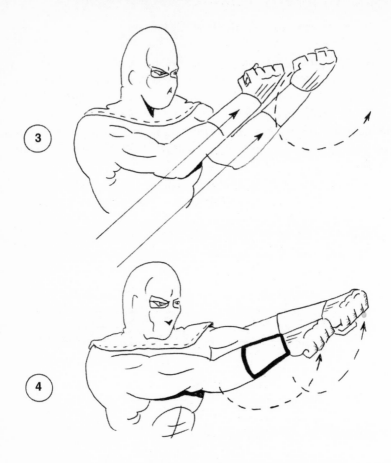

Figure 57C and D

(3) Pulling your extended fists back in towards your chest, strike upwards with *Double "Upper-Cut" Strikes*.

(4) Pulling your extended fists back in towards your chest, turn your fists *first down and then upwards* to strike with *Double "Snake-Fist" Strikes*.

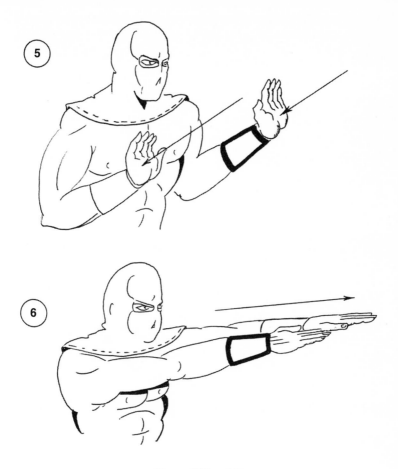

Figure 57E and F

(5) Open your fists as you pull them back to your chest.

(6) Strike forward (at eye level) with *Double Spear Hand Strikes*.

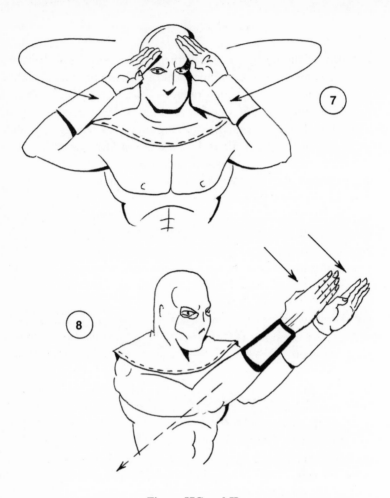

Figure 57G and H

(7) Pulling your Extended Open Hands in towards your forehead,

(8) Strike *forward and down* with *Double Sword Hand "chops"* (targeting a foe's neck and/or collarbones). Immediately upon "striking" his collarbones, draw your Open Hands back to your sides at chest level. *Note:* To complete this "kata" (form), *breathe out slowly and forcefully* as you "press" your open hands down . . . and relax. End.

Trí Thu: Grappling

The rule of thumb is that the further we can stay away from an enemy the safer we remain. Thus, striking an enemy down with a projectile weapon — from long range — is generally preferable to wrestling around on the floor with him. Likewise, striking an attacker with feet and hands is also preferable to having to match him muscle for muscle while rolling around on the ground.

However, since 90% of one-on-one encounters end up in grappling situations, most on the ground, the thorough martial artist is wise to add as much grappling science as possible to his arsenal.

In Cao Dai Pha Do, the term used for "grappling" in general is *Trí Thu,* a word that means both "spider" and "a spider's web." The underlying meaning here is obvious: to grapple fiercely, with an attitude and adroitness that makes our foe think we have eight arms and legs and/or that we are trapping and binding him up in a spider's web.

Wrestling, when applied specifically to combat, is *Chien Dau.* General, sport wrestling is *Danh vay,* and a wrestler, *Do Vat.* Interestingly, the word *Vat* means a "leech," as in something that latches onto you and won't let go.

While it might at first appear that the grappling technique requires muscles (always an asset), in actuality, Cao Dai kung-fu specializes in techniques that work no matter how small *you* may be, no matter how formidable your opponent might first appear.

Your attacker comes to the party with a plan. He plans to step forward, hit you, retract his hand and/or his kicking leg, before then repeating this sequence until you are unconscious . . . or worse!

To prevent this from happening, you need to upset his plan with a plan of your own. And part of *your* plan may include a grappling counter maneuver: "locking-out" his knee, sweeping his leading foot out from under him, and/or block-striking and grabbing onto his extended arm before he has a chance to retract it.

Cao Dai grappling countermoves first get us out of the line of fire while simultaneously maneuvering us into an advantageous position from which to restrict and ultimately control our enemy's future movement, thus allowing us to effectively launch a counterattack with every tactic and technique in the grappler's arsenal: painful joint attacks, arm and leg breaks, and bone-shattering takedowns.

Our grappling options include the use of *Num* seizing technique restricting his freedom of movement; forceful block/striking (Remember: There are *no blocks* in Cao Dai kung-fu!) stunning his striking arm, preventing his "re-loading his guns" while simultaneously denying his leading leg a firm footing.

To the uninitiated, it looks like there are a gazillion grappler's maneuvers, locks, and throws.

While it is true there are endless *variations* when it comes to grappling, all grappling ultimately comes down to finishing a foe with either a "lock-out" or a stranglehold, the first attacking vulnerable joints, while the latter concentrates on cutting off blood flow (oxygen), literally draining the fight — and, when necessary, *the life!* — from our enemy.

Whatever the specific "finishing move" used, in the end grappling comes down to a "simple" course in "Traps" and "Takedowns."

Cho Hung: Trapping

Cho Hung are methods used for *stifling* a foe's attack, *seizing* control of him, and/or *shifting* him into a position where he cannot continue his assault.

(1) **Shifting**. Our attacker expects us to "be there" when he gets there; in other words, he's already calculated where we will be standing when his punch or kick or weapon finally connects with us.

Our job, of course, is *not* to be there, to suddenly shift out of the way an instant before his attack connects, causing him to overextend himself, stumble, and hopefully fall — *hard*.

Shifting helps you — literally — "go out of your way" to "help" your attacker overextend himself, stumble, and fall — *hard!*

Review Figures 10 through 12 on *Lang tranh* shifting.

———

Evading an enemy's attack is also sometimes referred to as *Tro* (to "dodge," "evade"), and as *Ban quanh*, to "circle" around an opponent, to shift into an advantageous "position" from which to counterattack.

(2) **Stifling**. As your foe attacks, *stifle*, i.e., interrupt his forward momentum, by "locking-out" and/or breaking the knee of his lead leg with a "Chinese Cross Kick." (See Figure 23.)

You can also stifle his forward movement by sweeping into his leading leg with a low-level "Roundhouse Kick." (See Figure 35.)

A well-timed Elbow Strike (or any forceful blow) will stun his attacking arm (or leg), preventing it from retracting, giving you time to seize the stunned limb.

Rule: Having made initial contact with a foe, keep contact, either "collapsing" into him with multiple counterstrikes or else applying a grappling maneuver designed to literally take him down and out.

Always remember: "Kick on the break."

(3) *Num:* **Seizing**. Having stifled your foe's attack momentum, you are then free to seize a hold on him.

Remember that your attacker plans to strike you, retract his punching arm and punch again. But, by seizing his arm (or kicking leg), you not only prevent him from retracting and "reloading" his weapon, you also pull him off balance.

This is called *Om lay* in Vietnamese, "seizing hold of and clinging to" an enemy in order to upset his attack plan and timing.

Correctly seizing a hold on an opponent opens up new avenues of counterattack.

Figure 58A
Through the Arch Positioning

(1) Step forward *diagonally* to meet your opponent's punching
attack.
(2) Simultaneously, *strike* up into your attacker's punching arm
with a "Rising Block," creating "an arch" from the juncture
of your arm with your foe's arm.

Figure 58B

(1) Seizing hold of your foe's blocked arm, *step through the "arch" and pivot back into your foe's "centerline."*
(2) From this position, launch counterstrikes with the elbows . . .
(3) Hands . . .
(4) and Rear kicks and sweeps. (See Figure 73.)

Cho Hung literally means "a hollowed-out place." Thus, in Cao Dai Pha Do we use more than just our hands to trap an attacker. For example, we can trap his punching arm in our armpit, using "the Eagle's Nest" technique. (See Figure 59.)

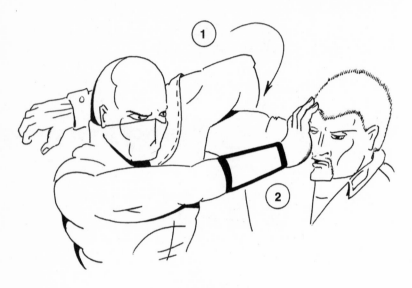

Figure 59
Eagle's Nest Trapping Technique

(1) Having blocked your attacker's arm with an outside block, circle your arm around his attacking arm, trapping it under your armpit and "locking-out" his elbow.
(2) Having trapped your attacker's arm, finish him with follow-up strikes and/or a takedown.

These techniques are also known as *Cho Trung* techniques.

We can likewise trap an attacker by draping our arm over his punching arm, "catching" it with our shoulder after "slipping" his punch.

Figure 60
Shoulder Slip-n-Lock

(1) As your attacker's punching arm passes harmlessly past your head, over your shoulder, circle your arm up and over his attacking arm while you simultaneously . . .

(2) Pivot and *drop your weight*, breaking his arm.

Still another arm-trap technique blocks/redirects our attacker's punch into the crook of our elbow.

Having trapped his arm, we are then free to counterattack, e.g., *break his arm!*

FYI: Western Cao Dai Pha Do students call this technique "Chinese Baseball," after the way the "ball" (foe's fist) is redirected and "caught" in the "catcher's mitt" elbow crook of the arm.

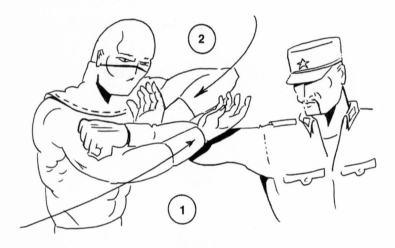

Figure 61
Chinese Baseball

(1) Using a "Cross-body Palm-Block," deflect your foe's attacking arm, clamping/trapping his wrist in the crook of your contracting elbow.
(2) Having trapped his arm, counterattack with strikes (e.g., Back-Fist) to his face.

Having successfully maneuvered yourself out of the line of fire and into an advantageous position, you are now free to seize a hold on your opponent (his arm, clothing, etc.), and are free to counterstrike your foe and/or apply a hold/lock/*break*, a takedown/throw, or a combination of all of these.

(4) *Ba:* **Lock-outs and Holds**. Not to denigrate fine grappling-oriented arts such as *jujutsu* and *aikido*, each of which have dozens of joint locking techniques, but joint locks basically come down to two types: wrist and hand twists and locks (which also apply to ankles), and elbow lock-outs, aka "Arm bar" (which can also be used to lock-out the knee).

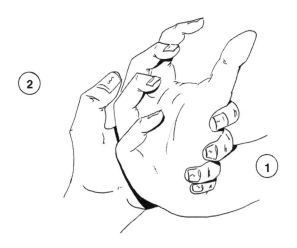

Figure 62
Wrist-Lock

(1) Seizing a grip on the "thumb pad" of your foe's hand,
(2) Forcefully jamb your own thumb into the back of his hand as you forcefully twist his wrist around and down. *Note:* Augment this wrist-lock with counterstrikes and/or with a take-down technique.

Figure 63
Arm Bar

(1) Seizing a hold on your attacker's extended arm at the wrist, *pull* the wrist towards you while you simultaneously . . .
(2) Rotate his arm to *extend and expose his elbow.*
(3) Strike into his extended elbow, forcing him to the ground and/or breaking his arm.

As mentioned, martial arts overall is 90% positioning. Likewise, grappling is also 90% positioning.

Shifts, pivoting and other "Methods of Movement" are all designed to put us in the best possible position from which to seize our opponent, in preparation for counterstrikes and/or takedowns.

FYI: The "Hold" Rule: *Never hold!*

Having successfully trapped your attacker's arm or leg, *break it.*

If the situation is serious enough to put someone into a painful wristlock or arm lock, it's probably serious enough to *break* that arm.

Its paw caught in a trap, a wild animal chews off its leg in order to escape certain death at the hands of the approaching hunter. Where your own safety and the safety of your loved ones is concerned, always assume your enemy is a "wild animal." In a kill-or-be-killed situation wouldn't *you* break your own arm in order to save your life?

We never know when we will find ourselves in a threatening situation that demands *Nhe rang*, literally "to show one's teeth," to show what we are made of, to use our determination to master the situation.

To kill or be killed.

FYI: If such "tough" talk threatens your comfortable white bread Western sensibilities, remember that Cao Dai kung-fu is the end product of over 1,000 years of constant warfare. The tactics and techniques taught in Cao Dai kung-fu have been tested in a thousand battles . . . and those tactics and techniques taught today were passed along by the *survivors* of those battles.

We live in especially troubling times. Steel yourself to do what must be done.

However beautiful your particular martial art, never forget the "martial" part.

Train with realism. Create realistic combat scenarios in your mind, the more *violent* and *terrifying* those images the better.

The harder the whetstone, the sharper the knife.

Example: Two or more psychopaths wielding box-cutters stand between you and the cockpit door, two psychopaths between you and you ever seeing your loved ones again.

Do you need a harder scenario than this on which to sharpen your wits and hits?

––––––

(5) *Siet Co:* **Strangleholds**. Having seized a hold on our attacker, it is a simple matter to shift-pivot him into an *Om co* stranglehold. (See Figures 64A and 64B.)

Figure 64A

Om co Stranglehold/Takedown

(1) Seizing a hold on your opponent at the lapels, *push* his one
shoulder back while *pulling* his opposite shoulder towards
you.

(2) Take a *step back* as you *push-pull* your opponent completely
around and off-balance.

Figure 64B

(1) Having push-pulled (pivoted) your opponent completely around, your pushing arm slides up and around his throat (jamming your forearm into his throat).

(2) Simultaneously, your "pulling" arm seizes a grip on your "pushing" arm, completing your stranglehold.

(3) Finish this technique by dropping your weight, pulling your victim back and down. If necessary, augment this technique by stomping onto the back of your victim's knee.

Such strangleholds are also called *Tran* for the way a strangler drops onto his victim like a deadly "boa constrictor."

Cao Dai warriors learn various strangleholds, both for use in taking out sentries during field combat operations and when fighting face-to-face with a foe.

For example, during the initial clash with a foe, it is a simple matter to block/strike his attacking arm and easily slip yourself into a "Half-Strangle" position:

Figure 65
Half-Strangle Takedown

Any forceful hold on an opponent's neck (cutting off blood flow-oxygen to the brain) sends him spiraling into unconsciousness within 30 seconds.

However, care must always be taken not to leave yourself open to counterattacks while applying your stranglehold. For example, the double-handed *Sam* "Crab" quickly "incapacitates" an attacker. But, apply this stranglehold only after your initial strike to his throat and to the base of his skull.

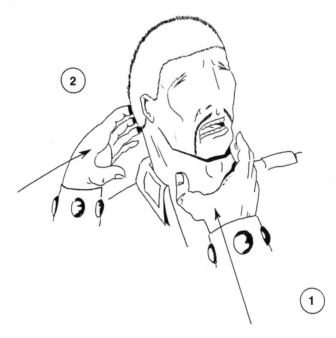

Figure 66
Sam Crab Strangle

(1) Strike into your opponent's larynx (front of the throat) with a "Tiger's Mouth Strike" while you . . .
(2) Simultaneously strike into the back of his neck ("Atlas and Axis") with a second "Tiger's Mouth." *Note:* Augment this technique by *pivoting* around and away from your opponent after applying this stranglehold.

Ropes, wires, and other tools are used as strangling weapons by Cao Dai warriors. (See *"Bat Am: Combat with Weapons."*)

FYI: Much-feared for their mastery of strangulation techniques, the ancient *Thuggee* cult terrorized India up into the 19th century. For a complete history of this cult and a complete training course in *Thuggee* combat, read *The Ancient Art of Strangulation*, by Dr. Haha Lung, Paladin Press, 1995.

Phurong: Takedowns

Phurong means "Phoenix" in Vietnamese. This mythical creature is perfect to represent the Cao Dai grappling takedown technique. Appearing dead, the Phoenix suddenly blazes back to life, consuming anyone standing too close!

Like the "guerilla fighter" he is, the Cao Dai grappler knows that by "giving ground" he can draw his over-eager opponent into an ambush from which there is no escape.

When his opponent *pushes*, he *pulls*.

His opponent *pulls*, he *pushes*.

His opponent rushes forward in a rage, the Cao Dai warrior calmly shifts and *pivots*.

Mixed with *shifting*, *stifling*, and *seizing*, this Push-Pull-Pivot strategy allows the Cao Dai warrior to outmaneuver any opponent — no matter their size.

Figure 67A
Wheel Throw

(1) Seizing a hold on your opponent's lapels (or his long hair!),
    pull him forward and down while you simultaneously . . .
(2) Strike into his midsection with a forceful Front Thrust Kick
    as you *begin to fall backwards.*

Figure 67B

(3) Still gripping your opponent, continue your fall backwards as
you *thrust upwards with your foot*, sending your opponent
flying! *Note: Do not release your hold*, instead roll completely over, coming to rest *straddling* your opponent's chest.
Finish him from this position.

This is the well-known "judo principle," aka "investing in loss."

To repeat: Your opponent pushes — you pull. He pulls — you
push. He surges forward — you adroitly pivot and he goes flying!

All *Phurong* moves are designed to unbalance a foe, sweep his
feet out from under him, and finish him off by maneuvering him
into a deficit position where he will be unable to continue his attack,
his pursuit, and/or his miserable life!

Now this is where Cao Dai kung-fu parts company with other
grappling "arts" such as sporting judo and aikido's insistence on
"becoming one with your attacker."

In Cao Dai kung-fu, you deliberately *slam* your attacker to the
ground and *finish him*, knocking him unconscious, injuring him
and/or otherwise assuring yourself he will not be able to get back up
and resume his assault.

You owe your enemy nothing. He has already made his choices in life — the *wrong* choices.

Study to survive, so you can make better choices.

———

The particular takedown technique you use against your attacker is determined by whether you are in front of him or behind him, e.g., taking out a sentry.

(1) **Front Takedowns**

Figure 68
Kick-Through Takedown

(1) As your opponent attacks, avoid his initial punch by stepping forward diagonally and kicking forward into his leading leg, toppling him forward to the ground.

(2) Augment this technique by striking into him as you "pass."

Figure 69
Twist-Down Takedown Technique

(1) Blocking your foe's initial attack, strike into his jaw with a Palm-Strike.
(2) Simultaneously, seize a grip on his hair, *pulling* at the same time you *push* against his jaw, twisting him around and down.
(3) Augment this "twist-down" by pivoting your leading leg back and around.
(4) Augment this technique by sweeping his leg out from under him.

Figure 70
Leg Draw Takedown

(1) Squatting in under your attacker's punching arm, Palm-Strike down into his leading knee.
(2) Simultaneously pull his lower leg up, "locking-out" his knee and toppling him to the ground. *Note:* Retain your grip on his leg and "finish" with a technique from Figure 76.

Figure 71A
Double Front Sweep Combination

(1) Strike forward with a low-level "Roundhouse" kick designed to sweep your opponent's lower leg out from under him. (See Figure 35.)

Figure 71B
Iron Broom Sweep

(1) Sweeping your opponent's leading leg out from under him
    (or if he raises his leading leg, successfully avoiding your
    initial sweep), immediately drop your leading/sweeping leg's
    knee to the ground.
(2) Balanced on your dropped knee, pivot 180° as you swing
    (arc) your *rigid* rear leg completely around towards the front,
    sweeping your opponent's second leg out from under him
    with an "Iron Broom" sweep. (See Figure 89.)

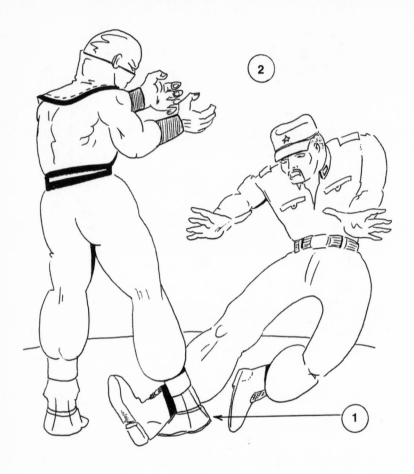

Figure 72
Leg Pull Takedown Technique

(1) At close quarters with your opponent, as you pull away, hook
your leading foot behind his leading foot and jerk your foot
towards you, upsetting his balance.
(2) Augment this sweep by pushing/striking against your opponent's upper body. *Note:* This technique is in keeping with
the *Cao Dai Pha Do* rule to always kick (or otherwise strike)
when breaking contact with an opponent.

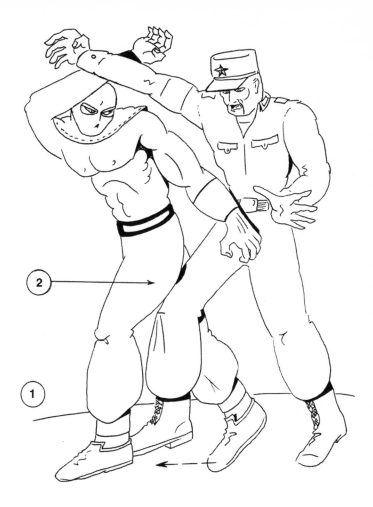

Figure 73
Fat Man Takes Your Chair

(1) Position yourself in close to your opponent, hooking one of
    your feet *behind* your opponent's calf.
(2) Suddenly jerk your hooked foot forward at the same time
    you squat, *sitting down onto your opponent's trapped leg*,
    toppling him to the ground.

(2) **Rear Takedowns**

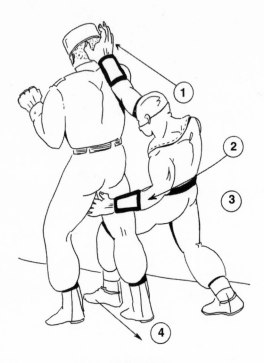

Figure 74
Tiger-Pull Takedown

(1) Approaching under your foe's "line-of-sight" from behind, strike/seize him with a forceful Palm-Strike to his Atlas and Axis while . . .

(2) Simultaneously striking up into his groin with a reverse Sword Hand Strike. Immediately upon impacting with your Sword Hand, *grab* onto your foe (i.e., reach through his legs from behind to seize his belt in front, his testicles, or the inseam fabric of loose pants crotch, etc.).

(3) *Pull* back on his crotch, pulling his legs out from under him at the same time you *push* his head forward, smashing his face into the ground.

(4) Augment this technique by sweeping his leg(s) out from under him using a "Kick-Back" sweep.

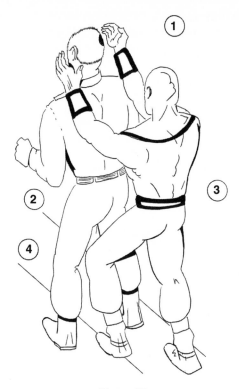

Figure 75
Buddha's Palm Takedown

(1) Approaching your foe from behind, under his line-of-sight, strike into both sides of his head by simultaneously slapping your *cupped hands* (aka, "Buddha's Palm") into his ears, stunning him.

(2) Simultaneous to your Buddha's Palm blows, strike up into his coccyx ("tailbone") with a solid Rising Knee Strike.

(3) Immediately upon striking into his ears, your Buddha's Palms turn into Tiger Claws and dig into your foe's eyes (and/or seize his long hair) as you *step back*, toppling him backwards to the ground.

(4) Augment this technique by stomping onto the back of his knee, breaking his balance before pulling him backwards. "Finish" with techniques from Figure 76.

(3) ***Gunzun Den:*** **Groundwork**. *Den* means snake and *Gunzun* is slang for a particularly nasty Southeast Asian krait snake that, once bitten, you take "two steps" and drop dead.

Snake is an apt representation for groundfighting since, on the ground, you want to immediately "slither" out from under your enemy's crushing heel.

A serpent also has a habit of "wrapping around" and sinking its fangs into anyone foolish enough to try bending down to pick it up.

Who's on the ground? You or him?

When he's on the ground: *Finish him.*

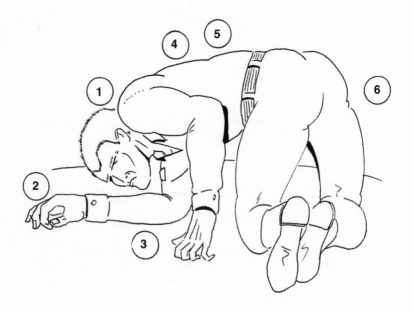

Figure 76
Ground-fighting Technique I

(1) Head and Neck: Stomp down onto, and kick up into, the head and neck (e.g., the Atlas and Axis).

(2) Fingers and Wrists can be injured/broken with stomps.

(3) Arms can be kicked out from under him to prevent his rising and/or can be broken with stomps.

(4) Spine: Strike anywhere along the exposed backbone with stomps and with heavy bludgeons. Kick up into the coccyx from behind.

(5) Ribs: Target the ribs and mid-section with forceful kicks.

(6) Legs and Feet: Target with kicks and stomps to break and prevent his rising again to his feet.

FYI: If kicking a man while he's down offends your sensibilities, you better hope your foe feels the same way when he has *you* on the ground!

When *you* are the one on the ground, *get up ASAP!*

However, while still on the ground, actively *fight back!* by kicking and trapping your attacker:

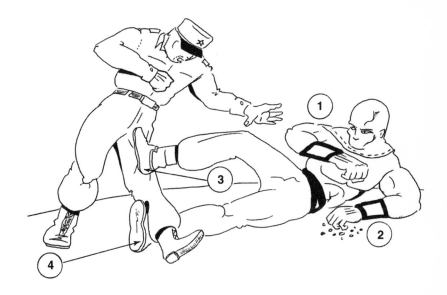

Figure 77
Ground-fighting Technique II

(1) Finding yourself on the ground, use one hand to block.

(2) Immediately, *fill your other hand*, picking up any weapon you can find (stones, sticks, dirt, etc.).

(3) Kick at your attacker with your feet, targeting his knees and lower body.

(4) Use your other foot to pull/lock his legs out from under him. Get to your feet ASAP. (See Figure 91.)

Rule: Any time your hand touches the ground *fill it with something*: dirt, a rock, a stick, etc.

Snowball is better than no ball.

Form and "Flow"

During combat we must be ever ready to "flow" into any gap in our enemy's defenses, while jealously guarding our own.

By the same token, we cannot afford to be content to wait for our enemy to "stumble," to mess up and give us such an opening. We must adopt strategies to *make him stumble*, giving us the opening(s) we need to finish the fight.

Interrupting our enemy's attack momentum while effectively counterattacking into him is the goal of combat.

We accomplish this by mastering ways of interrupting and interfering with his "flow" while simultaneously perfecting our own "flow."

Perfecting our own "flow" allows us to instantly take advantage of any "gap/space" between his first punch and his second, to attack him during that vulnerable instant between his kicking and his placing his foot firmly back on the ground, the opening created by his shifting from one stance to another.

"Sensing" a "gap" in his defenses, we instantly "flow" into it like water rushing through a suddenly open valve.

The tried-and-true method for developing this kind of natural "flow" is *correct repetition* of *correct form*.

"Practice makes perfect" *isn't* true, unless you are taught the *correct form* to practice in the first place.

Correct form practice gradually increases our speed and, ultimately our power.

Remember: Form + Speed = Power!

To return to our comparison of martial arts training to digging a ditch: Once *correct form* is learned, via repetition, our moves will then instinctively "flow" effortlessly along the lines of force we've learned, like water down that deep ditch we've dug, like electricity along the wires and circuits we've set in place.

It is relatively easy for a dedicated student to learn the various strikes, takedowns, and Methods of Movement required of Cao Dai Pha Do. The real challenge is to seamlessly weave these tactics and techniques together into a practical fighting "form."

This is the second meaning of "form:" a ritualized fighting exercise designed to help us develop "flow."

In Vietnam such "forms" are called *Mua vo*, "shadowboxing," and are identical to the "*kata*" fighting forms found in karate. These practice forms are also similar to the "shadowboxing" routines used in Western boxing . . . only longer and much more complex.

In past times and places where practicing martial arts was punishable by death, keeping a written account of outlawed martial arts teachings would have been suicide. Forbidden fighting styles were therefore systemized into forms that could easily be memorized and easily passed along from Master to student, from rebel to rebel.

Practice — and eventual mastery — of such fighting forms helps us develop the "flow" needed to smoothly move from one set of techniques to the next, until our foe is defeated.

The following *Mong Cop Mua Vo* "kata" comes from the Tiger cadre of Cao Dai Pha Do.

Mong cop means "Claw of the Tiger." This "kata" is known for its forceful "Tiger-Claw" striking of "soft" targets such as the eyes, throat, and groin, and for the way it mimics the tiger's "crouching" and "pouncing" with both high- and low-level attacks.

Most important, this "kata" teaches both *form* and *flow*.

———

In addition to the obvious strikes and takedowns, this form has dozens of "hidden" techniques that reveal themselves only to the diligent and truly dedicated.

Tiger-Claw Fighting Form

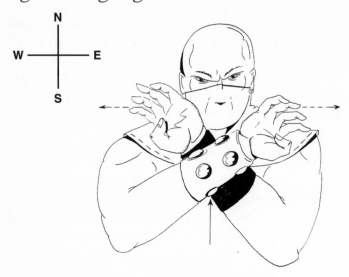

Figure 78A
Double Tiger-Claws

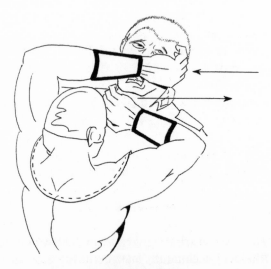

Figure 78B
Application of Double Tiger-Claws

Mong Cop Mua Vo

(1) Standing facing "North," your hands at your sides, feet together, bring both hands up from your sides to form a *Closed-Fist* (knuckles forward) *X-Block* (right hand in front of the left). Snapping open your fingers, turn your *Palms Forward* to form *Twin Tiger-Claws*.

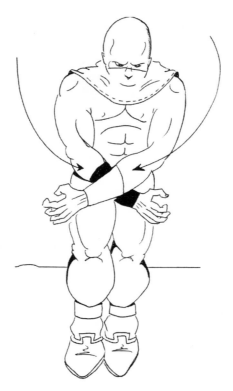

Figure 79
Carry Tiger to Mountain

(2) *Forcefully* separating your *Twin Tiger-Claws*, circle your *Arms Widely Outward And Down* until they cross at your navel. Simultaneously as your arms arc out and down, *Bend Slightly At The Knee*. Retain an *Upright Posture* throughout.

Figure 80
Tiger-Claw/Heel Stance

(3) As your *Tiger-Claws* cross at your navel, *Rise Out of Your Squat* and step your right foot out into a *Right Heel Stance* (*East*), simultaneously perform a *Right, Face-Level Descending Tiger-Claw Strike* (*East*).

(4) Repeat *Heel Stance/Tiger-Claw Strike* from Movement #3, *West*.

(5) Shifting *East* into a *Left Back Stance*, perform a *Right Palm-Up Block.*

Figure 81
Palm-Up Block/Back Stance

(6) Shifting your *Weight Forward* into a *Right Forward Stance*, perform a *Right Descending Tiger-Claw Strike* followed immediately by a *Left Descending Tiger-Claw Strike* from the same stance.

Figure 82
Descending Tiger-Claw/Front Stance

(7) Pull your *Rear-Left Foot* to your *Leading Right Leg's Knee* to form a *Right "Crane-Stance."* Simultaneously perform a *Right High-Level Vertical-Fist Strike East.*

Note: Some fighting cadres replace the "Crane-Stance" at this point with a "Cat-Stance."

Figure 83
Vertical Punch/Crane Stance

(8) Repeat Movements 5 through 7, *Mirror Image, West/Left*.

(9) Stepping your *Left Foot Behind Your Right Foot*, perform a *Tiger-Squat* (*North*). Simultaneously strike *North* with a *Right Low-Level Inverted Tiger-Claw Strike* (targeting groin) while your *Left Hand* forms a *Palm-Outwards Tiger-Claw* guarding your forehead.

Figure 84
Chinese Squat

(10) *Pivoting 180 Degrees* as you *Rise* from your Tiger-Squat into a *Left Forward Stance* (*North*), strike down with a *Left Descending Elbow Strike* that "collapses" into a *Left Descending Tiger-Claw Strike* (*North*) followed immediately by a *Right Descending Tiger-Claw Strike* (*North*), all in rapid succession.

Figure 85-A
Descending Elbow Strike

Figure 85-B
Tiger-Claw/Thigh Slap

(11) Stepping forward into a *Right Forward Stance* (*North*), perform a *Right High-Level Back-Fist Strike* followed immediately by a *Left Mid-Level Vertical "Reverse Punch"* from the same stance.

Figure 86
Leading Vertical Punch

(12) Placing your *Left Foot Behind Right*, perform a *Tiger-Squat* (*East*). Simultaneously your *Right Arm* performs a *High-Level Rising-Block* (i.e., *Left Tiger-Claw* guards forehead), while your *Left Hand Strikes* (*East*) with a *Low-Level Left Palm-Thrust*.

Figure 87
Tiger-Squat/Palm-Thrust

(13) Your *Left Foot Steps West* into a *Horse Stance*. Right forearm crosses left to form a *Low-Level X-Block*.

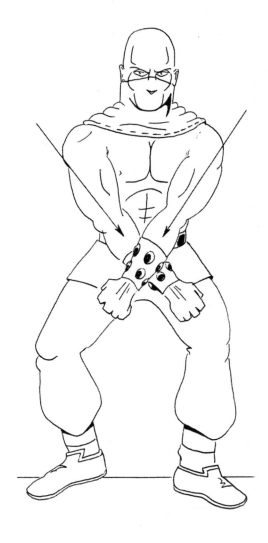

Figure 88
Horse Stance/X-Block

(14) Repeat Movement #12 *West/Left*, and then repeat Movement #13, stepping back (*East*) into a *Horse Stance*. End with *Low-Level Right-Over-Left X-Block*.

(15) Still in your *Horse Stance Facing North, Raise Your X-Block* to face-level and snap them open into *Tiger-Claws*. (Identical hand position in Movement #1.)

(16) Right *Knee Suddenly Drops To Floor* as you perform an *Inverted Right Tiger-Claw Strike* (*North*) and your *Left Tiger-Claw* guards forehead. (Identical hand position to Movement #9.)

(17) Balanced on your right knee, turn to face South and *Thrust Your Left Leg Outwards* (*South*) while you simultaneously *Reverse The Positions Of Your Tiger-Claws*. (Left strikes South, Right guards forehead.)

Figure 89
Knee Drop/Tiger-Claw/Sweep

(18) Still squatting, *Pull Your Left Leg In* as you simultaneously perform a *Left Cross-Body Block* paired with an *Upwards Tiger-Claw Strike* (*South*).

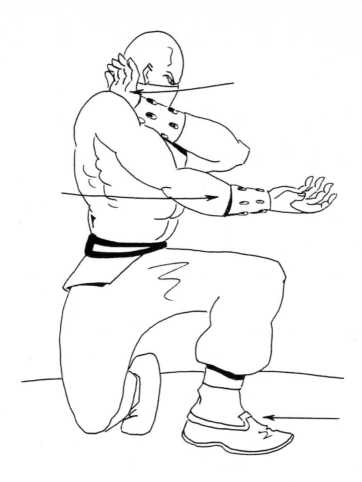

Figure 90
Cross-Body Block/Rising Tiger-Claw

(19) Shifting your *Weight Forward* onto your left leg, *Rise Quickly* to perform a *High-Level Right Back-Fist Strike* paired with a *High-Level Right Outside Crescent Kick*.

Figure 91

Rising with Crescent Kick and Back Fist

(20) As your right foot lands in a *Right Forward-Stance (South)*, perform a *High-Level Left Oblique Tiger-Claw Strike (South)*.

Figure 92
Oblique Tiger-Claw/Elbow Strike

(21) Stepping forward into a *Left Forward-Stance* (*South*), perform a *High-Level Right Oblique Tiger-Claw Strike*. (A mirror image of Movement #20.)

(22) Stepping forward into a *Right Forward-Stance* (*South*), perform a *High-Level Left Oblique Tiger-Claw Strike* (*South*). (Identical to Movement #19.)

(23) Bending forward, *Place Your Right Hand On The Floor* (*East*), pick up your *Left/Rear Foot* and, *Pivoting Right* (*West*), perform a *High-Level "Two-Point Heel-Kick"* (*West*).

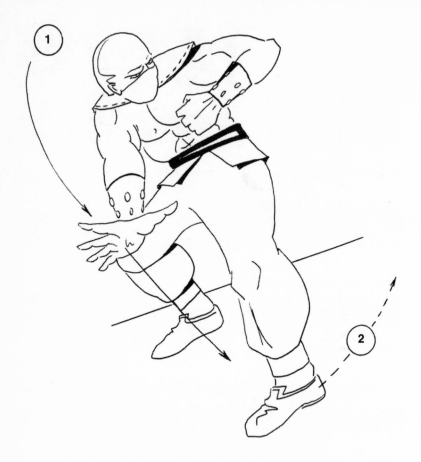

Figure 93A
Two-Point Kick

(1) Placing your leading hand onto the ground,
(2) Swing your rear leg back and up.

Figure 93B

(3) Target your opponent's head with a Heel Kick. (See Figure 35B.)

← (24) Placing your left kicking foot down into a *Right Back-Stance* (*West*), perform a *Mid-Level Double Sword-Hand Block*.

Figure 94A
Double Sword Hand Blocks (aka, "Crane Blades")

Figure 94B
Crane Spreads Wings I

(1) Block your attacker's punch by striking into his arm with
your "Crane Blades."

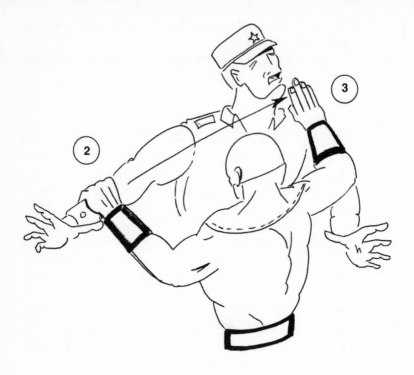

Figure 94C
Crane Spreads Wings II

(2) Having stunned his arm with your initial "Blades" block/ strike, seize a hold of his arm with your one hand while . . .

(3) Simultaneously striking into your foe with your second "blade." Target his throat. *Note:* This technique gets its name from the fact that the parting of your Sword Hands resembles a crane spreading his wings.

→   (25) Sliding both feet one step to the right (*East*) into a *Left Back-Stance* (*East*), perform a *Mid-Level Double Sword-Hand Block*. (This is the mirror image of Movement #24.)

↑   (26) Pulling your *Right Foot To Left Foot* (*Feet Together Facing North*), cross your forearms to form a *Chest-Level*

Closed-Fists X-Block, right-over-left. (This is the same position as Movement #1.)

(27) Glance left, then glance right. Open your palms, and drop them to your sides. End.

Application of Tiger-Claw Fighting Form

Movements 1 and 2: Having been seized from the front in a two-handed choke hold (or by an aggressor seizing your lapels), break your attacker's grip/hold by thrusting your crossed arms up between his attacking arms to strike into his throat, chin and/or face. (See Figure 78.)

Continue your counterattack by attacking his face with *Double Tiger-Claw Rakes Ripping* in the opposite direction: one claw raking across his throat, the other Tiger-claw raking across his eyes. (See Figure 79.)

Having delivered these simultaneous strikes, your Tiger-Claw hands continue up and out, pushing his arms out of the way.

Your arms then arc downwards as you bend at the knee, lowering your weight, as you strike into your opponent's "centerline" (face, solar plexus) with a *Forward Head-Butt*, even as your arms encircle his lower legs.

Pulling your arms back and up, topple your attacker to the ground.

Alternative Technique One: Having broken your attacker's choking grip, arc your arms up, out, and then back in, trapping ("locking out") his arms at the elbows.

Having locked out his elbow, strike into his face with a *Forward Head-Butt*. (See Figure 42.)

Alternative Technique Two: In lieu of encircling his legs, seize onto the tendons at the back of his knee with your Tiger-Claws. (See Figure 79.)

Alternative Technique Three: Having broken his choke/grip, your arms arc out and back in, attacking into the soft flesh of his sides with painful Tiger-Claw grips, unbalancing him.

Movements 3 and 4: Attacked by *Two Attackers*, one to your left, another to your right, immediately *Move Towards One of Your Attackers* (thus, away from the second attacker).

Counterattack into your closest attacker with a forceful *Tiger-Claw Block/Strike* to his face.

Turn immediately and strike into your second attacker with the same technique.

Movements 5 through 8: Turning back to your right-side attacker, strike into his attacking arm with a *Palm-Up Block* that doubles as a *Reverse Sword-Hand Strike*. (See Figure 22.)

Moving your weight into your attacker, instantly follow up your *Reverse Sword-Hand Strike* with a set of *Tiger-Claw Strikes* before finishing him off with a Vertical-Fist Strike.

Turning to your second attacker, repeat this *Three Strike Combination* in rapid succession.

Movements 9 through 11: Confronted by a punch (or by a high-level kick), immediately drop under the attacking hand by moving into a *Tiger-Squat*, guarding your head with your *Left-Hand Tiger-Claw* while forcefully striking into your attacker's groin (or respond to a kick by striking into the knee of the kicker's support leg) with an *Inverted Tiger-Claw*.

Immediately upon striking into your attacker's groin, continue into your counterattack by *Pivoting 180 Degrees* as you rise up and smash a *Descending Elbow Strike* down onto your attacker's upper body (targeting his collarbone, the bridge of the nose, etc.). (See Figure 85.)

In one smooth motion, follow this *Elbow Blow* with *Two Descending Tiger-Claw Rakes* (left hand then right) targeting his upper body (face, throat, or already broken collarbone).

Continuing the momentum initiated by these three rapid strikes, continue your "flow" forward into a *High-Level Right Back-Fist Strike* (targeting temple) followed by a *Left Vertical-Fist Strike* from the same *Right Forward Stance*. Target his "centerline" with this punch (solar plexus, throat, and face).

Movements 12 through 14: Attacked by three assailants (one right, one left, one ahead to center) immediately *Move to Intercept the Attacker* to your right by dropping into a *Tiger-Squat*, getting under his punching arm (and/or his high-level kick). Strike forcefully into his attacking limb with a *High-Level Right Rising Forearm*

Block while simultaneously counterattacking into his solar plexus (or, in the case of a kicking attack, into his supporting leg's knee) with a *Left Palm-Thrust*. (See Figure 9.)

As the center attacker executes a low-level kicking attack, you step left into a *Horse Stance*. Forcefully block "shock" and sweep aside his kicking leg with a *Powerful Low-Level X-Block* that doubles as a strike into the attacking leg.

Moving to meet your attacker on the left, repeat the successful defensive/counterattack just used on your right-side attacker (i.e., Tiger-Squat, Forearm Block/Strike, Palm Thrust).

Stepping Right, back into a *Horse Stance*, block the center attacker's low-level kick with a *Low-Level X-Block*.

Movement 15: Still in a *Horse Stance*, raise your arms, turning your *Low-Level X-Block* up into a *High-Level X-Block* (to block an attack aimed at your head).

Having blocked this attack by *Trapping Your Attacker's Hand at the Juncture of your Crossed Wrists*, now turn/flip your hands under and up at the wrists while opening them into *Twin Tiger-Claws*.

Your *Left Tiger-Claw Seizes Hold* of the attacker's arm. (See Figure 84.)

Movement 16: Still gripping your attacker's arm with your *Left Tiger-Claw*, *Drop Your Right Knee* to the ground as you strike into his groin (and/or lower body) with your *Right Hand* in an *Inverted Tiger-Claw Strike*. (See Figure 84.)

Alternative Technique: Having seized a grip on your attacker's arm, drop onto your *Right Knee* while simultaneously *Pulling His Arm Down* and *Striking* into his leading leg, "locking out" his knee, with a *Tiger-Claw/Palm Strike*, *Toppling Him Forward* (over your body). Augment this "take-down/throw" technique by "raising" your body up into the throw just as your "falling" attacker passes over your body. (See Figure 84.)

Movement 17: Still kneeling on your *Right Knee*, you are suddenly attacked by a *Stomping-Kick* rushing at you from your left (south).

You respond with a *Left Oblique Tiger-Strike* that sweeps aside the kicking leg while you simultaneously strike into his support *Knee* with a *Left Leg Side-Thrust Kick*.

Alternative Technique One: As your attacker rushes you, *Arc Your Left Leg Forward*, *Sweeping* his lead leg out from under him.

Alternative Technique Two: While you are in a prone position, your attacker attempts to punch down or grab down at you. You immediately seize a grip on his extended arm while counterattacking into his centerline with multiple *Side-Thrust Kicks* and/or *Heel Kicks*. (See Figures 77 and 89.)

Movement 18: Still kneeling on your *Right Knee*, having *Hooked Your Left Foot Behind* your attacker's leading foot, suddenly draw your *Extended Left Leg* in towards your body, *Sweeping Your Attacker's Lead Leg*, toppling him to the ground. Augment this take-down technique by "locking out" your attacker's lead knee and/or sweeping one or both of his legs out from under him with a *Right Inside-Outside Forearm Block* that doubles as an *Arm Sweep*. (See Figure 90.)

Movement 19: As you suddenly rise to your feet, strike into your attacker with a *Mid-Level Right Outside Crescent Kick* (targeting his ribs and/or kidneys) or with a *High-Level Crescent Kick* targeting his head. (See Figure 91.)

Movements 20 through 22: As your right kicking foot lands, surge forward into your stunned attacker with *Three Rapid-Fire Oblique Tiger-Claw Strikes*.

Alternative Technique: Your first Tiger-Claw strike *Blocks* an attacking hand *Inwards* as you step forward. Your Tiger-Claw then sweeps *Outwards*, back into your attacker's face, toppling him over your leg to the ground. (See Figure 92.)

Movement 23: From a *Right Front-Stance* (facing south), bend forward and place your right hand on the floor (east) as you *Whip Your Left Leg West*, striking your attacker with a *Left High-Level "Two-Point Heel Kick."* (See Figure 93.)

Alternative Technique: Performing this same Heel-Kick at low level turns it into a *Sweep*, toppling your attacker to the ground. (See "Iron Broom" sweep, Figure 71.)

Movements 24 and 25: Faced with attackers coming from the left and right, *Move to Intercept* the attacker on your right, countering his punching attack with *Double Sword-Hand Blocks/Strikes*.

Having stifled your left-side attacker, immediately *Slide to Your*

Right, intercepting your right-side attacker's punching attack with *Double Sword-Hand Blocks/Strikes*. (See Figure 94.)

Movements 26 and 27: Having finished off your multiple attackers, you return to your *X-Block* guarding position. (Movement #1.)

Glancing left and right, and seeing no danger, you drop your hands and relax.

Chapter Ten
Bat Am: Combat with Weapons

The Vietnamese have many names for martial arts weapons. For example, *Quan Khi* and *N Hung Khi* both mean "weapons" and "arms." *Cong Dau* literally translates to "bow and sword," but is often used to mean weapons in general.

Any warrior worth his salt — from streetfighters to guerilla fighters — knows that potential weapons are limited only by your determination — and desperation!

For instruction's sake, Cao Dai kung-fu recognizes five basic categories into which all weapons can be classified:

The Five Kinds of Weapons

Cao Dai kung-fu classifies all weapons into one of five basic kinds of weapons, depending upon their use:

(1) **Bludgeons** are used to batter down an enemy. These include a myriad of warclubs, sticks and staffs, as well as any heavy object you can fill your hand with and/or drop onto an enemy's head.

(2) **Bladed weapons** (Vietnamese *Cong*) includes everything from traditional knives (*Dao*) and swords (*Kiem*), to less conventional bladed weapons like broken pieces of glass, shards of rock and bone, razors, and box cutters.

Other bladed weapons include the *Ma Tau* scimitar favored by Tonkin pirates, hatchets (*Riu,* or *Tung*), spears (*Xa mau*), bladed hooks called *Queo*, a two-pronged pitchfork known as a *Chia*, and *May-may*, a collection of small bladed and spiked weapons similar to the *shuriken* "throwing stars" and caltrops used by Japanese ninja.

(3) **Flexible weapons** (Vietnamese *Day*) includes ropes, chains, whirling bludgeons, and wire (whether the trip-wire triggering a deadly booby-trap or the garrote wire suddenly around your neck!).

(4) **Hurling weapons** (Vietnamese *Nem*) include archery tools, the atlatl, throwing knives, and "ninja stars."

Modern firearms and explosives are also assigned to this category.

(5) **Psychological weapons** (See "*Am Hiem.*")

Figure 95
Queo and May-may, Weapons Use

There is much overlap of these weapon categories.

For example, Okinawan *nunchakus* ("numb-chucks") are techni-cally "bludgeons" yet are usually assigned to the "flexible weapons" category.

Likewise, a rock in your hand makes a handy "bludgeon" and/or "hurling weapon." Drop that same rock into a sock or tie it up in a scarf and it becomes an even more formidable "flexible weapon." (See "Silk/*Bao Thach*" in next section.)

A knife is a "bladed weapon" that can easily become a "hurling weapon."

When we run out of ammo, our rifle (a "hurling weapon") becomes a "bladed (bayonet) weapon" and/or a "bludgeon" by necessity.

Figure 96A

Adapting Unarmed Techniques to Weapon Use

(1) Replace your unarmed blocks . . .

(2) With weapon strikes.

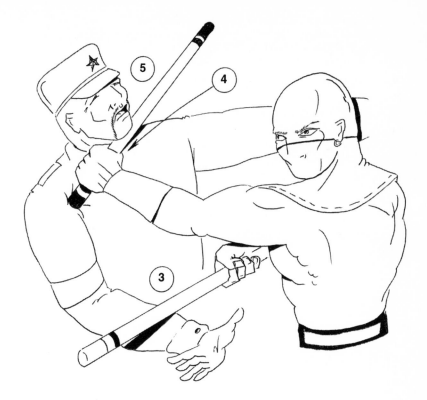

Figure 96B

(3) Block/Strike his attacking arm with your weapon the same
    way you do your unarmed blocks.
(4) Weapons strike "replaces" Hammerfist.
(5) Weapons strike "replaces" Sword Hand strike to throat and/or
    Forearm Strangle. (See Figure 40.)

FYI: The "secret" to mastering *any* weapon is to see it as a natural extension of yourself, not a foreign object you're holding.

Careful examination of many of your Cao Dai Pha Do "empty
hand" strikes will reveal how easily they can be adapted to weapons
use.

"The Eight Sounds"

Bat Am means "the Eight Sounds" and ironically the term was originally applied to the eight natural materials from which Vietnamese musical instruments are made: Stone, Wood, Bamboo, Gourds, Leather, Silk, Earthenware, and Metal.

Cao Dai warriors use this same term (i.e., "guerilla-speak") when talking about weapons since these are also the eight materials from which weapons can be crafted.

(1) **Stone** makes an excellent bludgeon and, thrown, becomes a Hurling weapon, and can also be used to construct flexible weapons.

(2) **Wood**: Depending on length and weight, any stick, from the smallest *Chiec dua* (chopstick), to a stout club and sharp stick, to a full-length staff can be used for fighting.

FYI: If you doubt the potential of a "simple stick," look up the statistics for how many injuries and deaths during America's Vietnam War were the result of *punji* (sharpened, shit-stained sticks used to construct booby-traps).

———

Generically, *Bao tong* is used when talking about a "walking cane," while *Dui* identifies a stick used for striking, i.e., "cudgel club."

Vietnamese stick-fighting is *Chong-gay* which literally means "to lean on a stick."

Cao Dai stick-fighting uses the same striking angles as does knife-fighting. In fact, bladed weapons instruction wisely begins with novices wielding wooden "knives" and "swords."

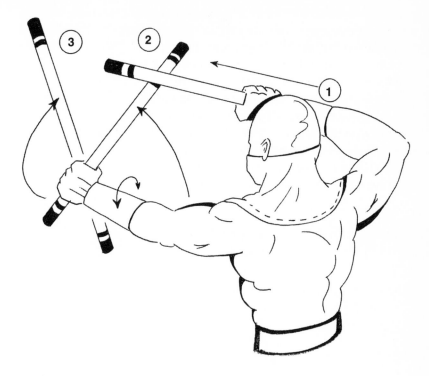

Figure 97
Basic Stick/Blade Attack Pattern

(1) Stab forward,
(2) High right strike,
(3) High left strike.

(3) ***Bamboo*** can be used in all the ways that other wood can. In addition, bamboo's flexibility makes it ideal for the construction of fighting sticks, "Bo"-staffs, and even crossbows. (Recall that the crossbow was invented by Highland 'Yards in Vietnam.)

Bamboo has been used to construct weapons ranging from booby-traps to blowguns (Vietnamese *Ong dong*).

(4) ***Gourds*** are used for carrying poisons and have even been packed with explosives to make impromptu grenades.

(5) ***Leather*** can be used for strangling and in the construction of booby-traps. It can also bind up an enemy and aid in the construction of flexible weapons (*Can day*).

The Vietnamese *Vut* (fighting whip) is made from leather, its tip augmented with a metal stud.

A popular ambush technique called "*Ai sat*" (literally "death by hanging," also called "Snake-in-tree") uses a braided leather noose to strangle a victim.

Figure 98A
Ai sat Ambush/Strangle

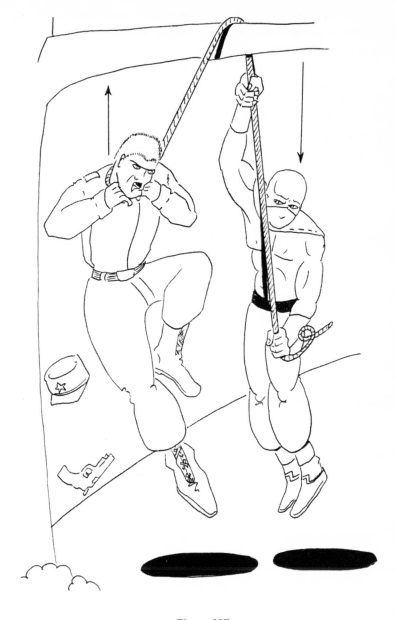

Figure 98B

(6) **Silk** can be used for strangling, as was proven by the dreaded *Thuggee* cult of India who specialized in strangling their victims with a silken scarf weighed down by a heavy coin. (Lung, 1995)

The *Boa Thach* (literally "Precious Stone") is a flexible bludgeon constructed by securing a stone (or other heavy object) inside a silken scarf.

A sub-system of martial arts known as *Can Dai* (literally "Turban and Sash") has been built around the art of fighting with scarves and other flexible weapons.

(7) **Earthenware** can be dropped onto an invader's head, and can be used to carry and construct explosives.

Apart from this literal use, the term "Earthenware" is used as a euphemism for attacking an enemy with poison and chemical agents. Can you say "Anthrax?"

(8) **Metal** has been used to construct weapons ranging from ancient swords down to modern firearms.

Chut Dinh: "Little Monsters"

Chut dinh means *"a little bit,"* referring to "small" weapons easily hidden on a fighter's body.

Japanese ninja called such weapons *tonki*. These include everything from a handful of sand or pepper we can toss into an enemy's eyes to small stabbing and cutting tools (dirks, *shuriken*, razors, etc.).

Cao Dai warriors also refer to these kinds of weapons as *Vo khi can chien*, "weapons of close combat."

———

It has been said, "The pen is mightier than the sword." But your pen remains a pen until your determination — and desperation! — decides it is a sword!

If you doubt the destructive power of such "little monsters," need we mention those "Nine-Eleven" box cutters again?

Chapter Eleven
Âm Hiem: Subterfuge and Stealth

"Covert operations are vital to your war effort." (Sun Tzu)

When a direct (*cheng*) assault won't work against our enemy, a more circuitous (*chi*) strategy is called for.

Many times throughout history the outcome of a bloody battle has been determined beforehand by an accidentally misplaced bit of information or, just as often, a deliberately dropped piece of *mis*-information.

Often a single piece of information spells the difference between the sweetest of victories and the bitterest of defeats.

In February, 1904, the Japanese destroyed the Russian fleet at Port Arthur (now called *Lu-shun*, China).

As a result of this surprise attack (repeated 35 years later at Pearl Harbor!) Japan ultimately won the 1904–1905 Russo-Japanese War and became a significant power in the Far East.

The outcome of the surprise attack on the Russian fleet is well documented.

What isn't as well known is that the Russian-born *British* spy (who occasionally worked for German Intelligence) named Sidney Reilly had given the Japanese detailed plans for Port Arthur, including the exact positions of Russian ships "trapped" in the harbor.

Reilly obtained this detailed information by hoisting a small Chinese boy aloft in a box-kite. A natural artist, the boy drew a complete layout of Port Arthur, which Reilly (with the blessing of his British handlers who had a vested interest in seeing the rival Russian fleet sunk) then passed along to his Japanese contacts.

Armed with this information, the Japanese made short work of the Russian fleet.

This is a perfect example of how battles — and even wars — are all too often won, not by the courage and sacrifice of warriors on the field, but by shady double-dealings that go on behind "the Black Curtain."

FYI: Just for the record, the British "using" the Japanese to destroy Britain's European rival Russia is an example of the ploy "Get a dog to eat a dog," or "The enemy of my enemy is my friend." (See *The Black Science: Ancient and Modern Techniques of Ninja Mind Manipulation*, Lung and Prowant, 2001, Paladin Press.)

————

Cao Dai warriors are schooled that there is *always* more to winning a confrontation than just physical prowess. Many battles are fought *in the mind*. In fact, Sun Tzu tells us that defeating an enemy without fighting is the greatest of accomplishments, i.e., defeating him without having to face him on an open battlefield where we are in the most danger.

The use of *Chi* strategy isn't a choice when it comes to a guerilla army, it is a necessity.

Vietnamese call this "mental element" of warfare *Cuoc dau tri*, "a duel of wits," and *Chien Tranh an nao*, "a war of nerves."

Thus, when open combat is futile, foolish, and fatal, *Quy ke*, the use of "stratagem" becomes the order of the day.

Therefore, to our already keen blade of physical fighting skills, we must add *Tam thuoc doc*, literally "a coating of poison," i.e., adding an element of "espionage" to our arsenal, special skills and special agents we can call upon when need be.

Dac Vien: Special Agents

"An army without spies is like a man deaf and blind." (*Chia Lin*)

Knowledge is power, and intelligence — both the innate kind and the gathered variety — is the key to unlocking Victory's stubborn chastity belt.

Cao Dai operatives specializing in espionage were/are known as *O Nhm*, "Black Crows," and are the equal of both the Chinese Moshuh Nanren and the Japanese ninja, from whom *O Nhm* undoubtedly looted many of their more effective techniques.

While fully capable of standing toe-to-toe with a foe, unlike uniformed Cao Dai militiamen, *O Nhm* preferred operating behind the scenes as *Do tham*, spies (aka *Do do*), quietly gathering information and carrying out covert operations.

Sun Tzu devotes an entire chapter in his *Ping Fa* to the recruitment and use of "special agents." These include one's own trained intelligence operatives and assassins, as well as defectors we can entice away from our enemy's camp.

Whenever possible, Cao Dai "spymasters" preferred to field their own dedicated and trustworthy agents.

When this was not possible, they resorted to hiring professional spies willing to sell information to the highest bidder, professional *Thich knach* assassins, and other criminals.

For example, a professional *Am Trom*, "Thief/burglar," might be hired to either "pull a job" (e.g., steal a valuable map or file), or else to teach his valuable skill to Cao Dai operatives.

Such "contract workers" were called *Mai Kiem* which literally means "to sell one's cheeks," in other words, a whore, a clear reference to their mercenary nature.

———

"Unless subtle, you can never get the truth from spies."
(Sun Tzu)

Special Skills

The more our skills, the more our options, the better our chances of coming up with the right solution.

Cao Dai warriors were/are encouraged to acquire abilities far beyond just physical fighting skills.

You never know which "special skill" might come in handy. This is particularly true of tactics and techniques specifically crafted to confuse an enemy. Collectively, these tactics and techniques are known as *Ao Canh*, "the Art of Mirage."

Ao Canh includes all the skills vital to espionage: infiltration, intelligence gathering, assassination, escape and evasion, as well as how to successfully attack an enemy at his weakest point — his *mind!*

The Art of Espionage

"Reliable intelligence cannot be obtained by conjuring 'spirits,' nor by petitioning the Gods, nor by comparing your present troubles to past triumphs, not even by mathematical calculation. Reliable intelligence can only be obtained from men who know firsthand the enemy's position and intent." (Sun Tzu)

Espionage revolves around two basic objectives: intelligence gathering and assassination.

In order to accomplish either of these two objectives, Cao Dai *Gian te*, "spies," are often required to learn special skills that will allow them to get close to their target (no matter whether that "target" is a computer disk, or a face framed in your crosshairs).

Getting close to your target is sometimes as "simple" as sneaking past his defenses, people and perimeters, and patiently waiting for your "target" to come within range.

Other times, such infiltration involves complex disguises, flawless document forgery, mastery of a foreign language, and a host of other skills.

For example, *Dan ban*, "the Art of Disguise," is a required course of study for Cao Dai *O Nhm*. This includes every form of disguise from altering your look and identity in order to gain entry into a heavily guarded installation only long enough to photograph classified information, to putting deep-cover "sleeper agents" in place for years.

But reaching your target means little if you get caught in the process.

Getting caught = getting interrogated/*tortured* = the possibility you will inadvertently endanger your comrades. Therefore, *capture is not an option.*

Mastery of *Escape and Evasion* (*An Biet*, literally "to vanish without a trace") was also required training for *O Nhm*.

Like other "special forces" cadres, *O Nhm* were expected to master *Hoa trang* in order to "camouflage" their daytime activities, and master *Da dau*, "Night movement," in preparation for *Da Chien*, night combat.

Bính Van: The Black Science

It's apropos that the Vietnamese word *Tung* means both "knife" and "mouth."

To defeat an enemy physically gets the job done. However, it has often been said that "Reputation spills less blood." A dagger of fear can kill quicker than a dagger of steel. The right word in the right ear accomplishes much, and often wins a battle before that battle begins.

Doubt is the doorway to death. Make a man doubt himself, doubt his abilities and the validity of his battle plans, make him doubt his best friend, and you have already defeated him. Read *Othello*.

Planting doubt, false information, masterful propaganda, and out-and-out lies all fall under the Art of Suggestibility (*Am thi tinh*) and includes the spreading of information designed to confuse and panic the enemy.

Masters of this kind of psychological warfare are called *Nha thoi mien hoc*, literally "Hypnotists," for obvious reasons.

O Nhm mind-slayers know that somewhere within the *That tinh* "Seven Passions" — Joy, Anger, Sorrow, Fear, Love, Hate and Lust — can be found a foible or faux pas to trip up any of us.

———

The Vietnamese say life is *Cahn ton*, "a struggle for existence." The Vietnamese speak from experience.

On the battlefield of life, it is your experience — sweat and blood and prior study — that speaks for you.

Study to survive so that when your experience is called to speak for you, it sings loud a victory song, and not your funeral dirge!

Sources and Suggested Reading

Brewer, Cobham (1959), *The Wordsworth Dictionary of Phrase & Fable*, Wordsworth Editions, Ltd., London. Revised by Ivor H. Evans.

Dao Thu Hiem (1997), "Vietnamese Hybrid Faith," *Hinduism Today*, November, 1997, p. 47.

Dooley, George E. (2000), *Battle for the Central Highlands*, Ballentine, Del Rey, California.

Eliade, Mircea, Editor in Chief (1987), *The Encyclopedia of Religion*, Macmillan Publishing Company, New York.

Laqueur, Walter (1977), *Terrorism*, Little, Brown & Company.

Loewen, James W. (1995), *Lies My Teacher Told Me*, The New Press.

Lung, Dr. Haha (1995), *The Ancient Art of Strangulation*, Paladin Press, Colorado.

——— (1997A), *Assassin! Secrets of the Cult of Assassins*, Paladin Press.

——— (1997B), *The Ninja Craft*, Alpha Publications of Ohio.

——— (1998), *Knights of Darkness*, Paladin Press.

——— (2002), *Koopo-jutsu: The Lost Art of Bone-Breaking*, Publication pending.

Lung, Dr. Haha and Prowant, Christopher B. (2000), *Shadowhand: Secrets of Ninja Taisavaki*, Paladin Press.

——— (2001), *The Black Science: Ancient and Modern Techniques of Ninja Mind Manipulation*, Paladin Press.

Mushashi, Myamoto (1643), *A Book of Five Rings*, Miscellaneous translations in print.

Naito, Hatsuho (1989), *Thundergods: The Kamikaze Pilots Tell Their Story*, Translation Mayumi Ichikawa, Kodansha International, Tokyo.

Omar, Ralf Dean (1989), "Ninja Death Touch: The Fact and the Fiction," *Blackbelt*, September 1989.

―――― (1993), *Death on Your Doorstep: 101 Weapons in the Home*, Alpha Publications of Ohio.

―――― (2001), *Prison Killing Techniques: Blade, Bludgeon & Bomb*, Loompanics Unlimited, Washington.

Prowant, Christopher B. and Skinner, Dirk (2002), *X-Treme Boxing: Secrets of the Savage Street Boxer*, Paladin Press.

Skinner, Dirk (1995), *Street Ninja: Ancient Secrets for Mastering Today's Mean Streets*, Barricade Books, New York.

Smith, Lawrence (2000), *Do What Thou Wilt: A Life of Aleister Crowley*, St. Martin's Press.

Sun Tzu (500 BC), *Ping Fa/The Art of War*, Miscellaneous translations in print.

Time-Life Books (1995), *Southeast Asia: A Past Regained* (Lost Civilizations series), Time-Life Books, Virginia.

Vankin, Jonathan (1992), *Conspiracies, Cover-ups and Crimes: Political Manipulation and Mind Control in America*, Paragon House, New York.

Wilson, Robert Anton (1977), *Cosmic Trigger: The Final Secrets of the Illuminati*, New Falcon Press.